Discover the enchanting world of tea leaf & blossom
where ancient traditions meet modern wellness

Teas & Tisanes

Whispers of the Leaf

" In every drop, a secret sigh,
Of mountain mist and twilight sky.
A leaf's soft whisper in quiet streams,
Awakening worlds, of ancient dreams

GOPAL DWIVEDI

Dedication

To my grandfather who believed that

*"The Gods were meant to transcend...
to relish the divine infusions"*

To my loving dad who served him so...

सर्वेन्द्रियाणां जर्हन्ति तेजः आशास्यं पुरुषं पुण्यं एतन्मूलं विदुः सुधाम्।

Sarvendriyāṇāṁ jarhanti tejaḥ
Āśāsyaṁ puruṣaṁ puṇyaṁ
Etanmūlaṁ viduḥ sudhām।

Destroying the vigor of all senses,
Pleasing to the virtuous man,
They know the root of this as nectar (ambrosia).

"Bhagavad Gita"

Publisher : notionpress.com

Notion Press, Inc.
800, West El Camino Real #180,
California USA 94040

Notion Press Media Pvt Ltd,
#7, Red Cross Road,
Egmore, Chennai, Tamil Nadu 600008

Title : Teas & Tisanes : Whispers of the Leaf

First Addition : 2024
Published in India
ISBN : Mentioned at back cover page
Author : Gopal Dwivedi
Book Forward : Payalh Agarwwal

Forward

As a lifelong lover of tea and an entrepreneur deeply immersed in the world of this extraordinary beverage, I am thrilled to share my thoughts on this remarkable book. It is not just a collection of knowledge; it is a game-changer in how we understand and appreciate the humble tea leaf.

From the first sip to the last, tea has always been more than just a drink to me—it's a way of life. This book encapsulates that sentiment perfectly, taking us on a journey that bridges the rich traditions of tea with the innovations that are shaping its future. It offers a profound exploration into the art and science of tea, unveiling the true value and significance hidden within each leaf.

As I delved into the pages, I found myself repeatedly inspired by the depth of insight and the passion that the author brings to the subject. This is more than just a guide; it's a treasure trove of wisdom that elevates our understanding of tea to new heights. Whether you are a seasoned professional or someone just beginning to explore the world of tea, this book has something invaluable to offer. It is with great joy that I endorse this work, knowing that it will transform the way you experience tea, just as it has for me. May it inspire you to see beyond the ordinary and to discover the extraordinary in every cup.

Payalh Agarwwal : Teapreneur & Founder of ChaiOm

"The lady who has more tea than blood in her veins "

Acknowledgments

This book is the culmination of years of passion, experimentation, and love for tea, and it would not have been possible without the support and encouragement of many wonderful people.

First and foremost, I extend my deepest gratitude to my mother, Jaya, whose knowledge of herbs, spices, and flavors laid the foundation for my understanding of tea. Her guidance has been invaluable in this journey. To my wife, Priyanka, thank you for your patience and support as I explored and created various tea blends. Your willingness to be my taste-tester and your constructive feedback were crucial in refining these recipes.

I am also grateful to my family & friends Girish, Vinay, Karan, Isha, Rashmi,Uma, Akansha, Mansi, Haimee, Mihir, Yug, Heer, Purvai, Hiya & Myra for their critical feedback and suggestions. Your insights helped me view flavors with greater objectivity and enhanced the quality of this book.

A special thanks to Shaha Zhang, Founder of the International Tea Academy, for her invaluable inputs and for sharing her profound knowledge of tea. Your expertise has enriched this book in countless ways. I also want to acknowledge Mr. Rishav Kanoi, founder of Tea Trove, and Ms Paylah Agarwal, Teapreneur, whose tea samples and recipes made an indispensable contribution. Your generosity and support have been instrumental in bringing this book to life.

Lastly, to all the tea lovers and enthusiasts who have shared their stories, experiences, and love for tea, thank you for being a part of this journey. This book is for you.

With heartfelt gratitude,

Gopal Dwivedi

Preface

The aroma of freshly brewed tea has been a constant companion throughout my life, bringing with it a sense of comfort and nostalgia. Tea is more than a beverage; it is a thread woven into the fabric of my life, connecting generations and memories, moments of joy and reflection, and the simple yet profound act of sharing. As an acclaimed interior designer and an award-winning author of a book on tea recipes, my journey with tea has been both personal and professional, a love story that began in my childhood and has blossomed into a lifelong passion.

Growing up in the enchanting city of Udaipur, often called the "City of Lakes," my unpretentious family was the cornerstone of my existence. With my loving grandparents, parents and three sisters, our home was always bustling with activity, laughter, and, of course, the comforting aroma of tea. My earliest memories are filled with the sight of my father serving afternoon tea to my grandfather. It was a daily ritual, a sacred moment that encapsulated the essence of our familial bonds. I vividly recall my grandfather's words, spoken with a twinkle in his eye: **"This tea is so good that even the gods would wish to descend from heaven to taste it."**

My father was the architect of these cherished tea moments, but it was my mother who was the magician in the kitchen. A phenomenal cook, she had an innate ability to transform simple ingredients into culinary masterpieces. To this day, her magical tea masala recipe continues to make our tea unique and tasty. Later in this book, I will surely share the secret tea masala recipe of my mother. As a child, I absorbed her techniques and recipes almost osmotically, watching her deft hands and listening to her sage advice. Cooking became second nature to me, a skill I carried forward into adulthood, where I now prepare meals for my own family—my wife and daughters. Yet, amidst all the culinary adventures, tea remained a constant, an integral part of our daily lives.

Tea punctuates the rhythm of my day. Morning tea at home is a gentle awakening, a moment of calm before the day's hustle and bustle. At the office, tea serves as a companion during busy meetings, providing clarity and focus. Evenings often find me at a local tapri, savoring a cup of chai amidst the chatter and camaraderie of friends and strangers alike.

On special nights, when guests grace our home, tea is the star of the evening, a symbol of hospitality and warmth.

The idea of writing a book dedicated to tea was a natural progression of my love for this timeless beverage. But I knew that to do justice to such a topic, I needed to immerse myself deeply in the world of tea. Over the years, I have tasted and experimented with more than a hundred types of tea and tisane. Each variety brought its own unique flavor profile, history, and cultural significance, enriching my understanding and appreciation of tea.

This journey culminated in the creation of my own tea brand, XOXO—Love and Hugs in a Cup. XOXO is more than a brand; it is a manifestation of my journey, a tribute to the countless cups of tea that have shaped my life. Each blend in the XOXO collection is crafted with love and a deep respect for the art of tea-making, designed to offer a moment of solace, joy, and connection.

Tea is a universal language, a bridge that connects people across cultures and generations. It is a symbol of hospitality, a gesture of kindness, and a source of comfort. Whether you are a seasoned tea connoisseur or a casual drinker, I hope this book inspires you to explore the world of tea with curiosity and passion. May it encourage you to create your own tea rituals, to share a cup with loved ones, and to find joy in the simple act of brewing and savoring tea.

In writing this book, I have poured my heart and soul into each page, much like the way one pours a perfect cup of tea. It is my sincere hope that "My Personal Story of Tea" resonates with you, that it brings a smile to your face and warmth to your heart. So, make yourself a cup of your favorite tea, find a comfortable spot, and join me on this journey. Together, let us celebrate the magic of tea—its flavors, its stories, and its ability to bring people together.

Thank you for allowing me to share my personal tea experiences with you. Enjoy the journey, and may each cup of tea you brew be filled with love, joy, and a touch of magic.

Index

"This page is brewing its thoughts... just like your perfect cup of tea."

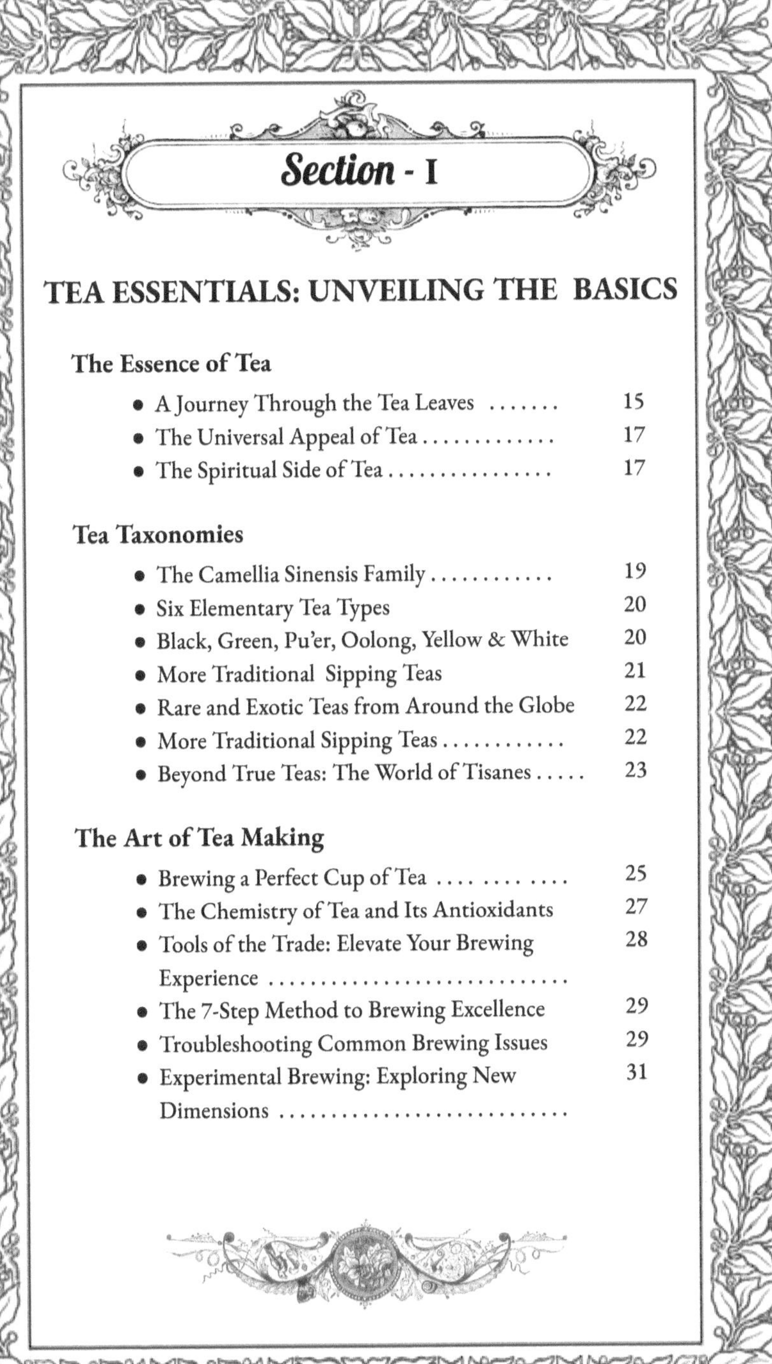

Section - I

TEA ESSENTIALS: UNVEILING THE BASICS

The Essence of Tea

Tea Taxonomies

The Art of Tea Making

TEAS AND TISANES : WHISPERS OF THE LEAF

"A moment of stillness—like waiting for the kettle to whistle."

1.1 - THE ESSENCE OF TEA

A JOURNEY THROUGH THE TEA LEAVES

am a small, delicate tea leaf, whispering to you from the heart of the misty mountains of ancient China. My story is as old as civilization itself, beginning with legends and flowing through centuries like a winding river. Sit back, relax, and let me unfold the tale of my origins and evolution.

Once upon a time, in 2737 B.C., there was a Chinese emperor named Shen Nong. He was a wise man, a herbalist, and a lover of nature. One day, as he was boiling water under the shade of a majestic Camellia sinensis tree, a few leaves, like myself, drifted down and landed in his pot. Intrigued by the aroma wafting up from the brew, he decided to take a sip. And so, the first cup of tea was born. He marveled at its refreshing taste and its calming yet invigorating effects. From that moment on, tea became an integral part of Chinese culture, valued not just for its flavor but also for its medicinal properties.

As centuries passed, my popularity spread beyond the imperial courts to the common folk. During the Tang Dynasty (618-907 A.D.), a man named Lu Yu, affectionately known as the Sage of Tea, wrote the "Cha Jing" or "The Classic of Tea." This seminal work detailed everything from the cultivation of tea plants to the art of tea preparation and drinking. It was an ode to the simple yet profound beauty of tea, and it solidified my place in Chinese society.

But my journey didn't end there. I was destined to travel across continents, breaking barriers and weaving myself into the fabric of various cultures. In the 8th century, Buddhist monks from Japan visited China and were enchanted by the tea ceremonies they witnessed. They brought tea seeds back to Japan, where tea cultivation began to flourish. The Japanese developed their own unique tea culture, epitomized by the elegant and tranquil tea ceremony, or "chanoyu," which became a spiritual practice centered around mindfulness and harmony.

Meanwhile, in the 16th century, European explorers and traders began to take notice of me. Portuguese and Dutch merchants were among the first to bring tea to Europe. At first, I was a rare and exotic commodity, enjoyed mainly by the aristocracy. However, as the British East India Company established trade routes with China, I began my love affair with England. By the 17th century, tea had become a beloved beverage in British society. The British added their own twist by introducing the practice of afternoon tea, a delightful ritual of sipping tea while enjoying dainty sandwiches and pastries.

One of the most notable figures in my history is Catherine of Braganza, the Portuguese princess who married King Charles II of England in 1662. She brought her love of tea to the English court, and her influence helped popularize tea among the British nobility. Soon, tea drinking became a fashionable pastime, and tea gardens and tea houses sprang up across London.

As my popularity soared, the British sought to control my production and trade. In the 19th century, they turned their attention to India, where they established vast tea plantations in Assam and Darjeeling.

This marked a new chapter in my story, as Indian teas, with their robust and distinctive flavors, became a cornerstone of the global tea industry. The British also introduced tea to Sri Lanka, formerly known as Ceylon, where tea cultivation thrived in the lush highlands.

But my journey didn't stop in Europe and Asia. I found my way to the New World, where tea played a pivotal role in one of the most significant events in American history. In 1773, American colonists, frustrated by British taxes on tea, staged the Boston Tea Party, a bold act of defiance that helped spark the American Revolution. Though I was tossed into the harbor that night, my symbolic importance was far from diminished.

Throughout the centuries, I have continued to evolve and adapt to changing tastes and cultures. Today, there are countless varieties of tea, from the delicate white teas of Fujian to the smoky lapsang souchong, from the fragrant jasmine teas to the robust and malty Assam teas. Each type of tea has its own unique story, shaped by the terroir, the climate, and the traditions of the people who cultivate and enjoy it.

As I whisper my tale to you, I'm reminded of the many hands that have carefully plucked me, the skilled artisans who have processed and refined me, and the countless tea lovers who have savored my essence. I've been a silent witness to history, a humble leaf that has brought comfort, joy, and a sense of connection to people around the world.

So, the next time you brew a cup of tea, take a moment to reflect on my journey. From the ancient mountains of China to your teacup, I've traveled far and wide, carrying with me the whispers of centuries past. I am more than just a beverage; I am a bridge between cultures, a symbol of hospitality, and a testament to the enduring human spirit.

And as I steep in hot water, releasing my flavors and aromas, I invite you to join me in this timeless ritual. Let us share a moment of tranquility and appreciation for the simple yet profound pleasure that is tea. For in every sip, there is a story waiting to be told, a whisper of a leaf that has traveled through time and space to bring you a taste of history.

The Universal Appeal of Tea.

I am a humble tea leaf, and my journey transcends borders, cultures, and generations. From the bustling streets of Mumbai to the serene tea houses of Kyoto, I serve as a unifying thread in the tapestry of human connection. I am a cultural cornerstone, a source of comfort, and a symbol of hospitality that resonates with people across the globe.

A serendipitous moment with Emperor Shen Nong in China revealed my delightful infusion. This simple accident not only birthed a beverage but also set in motion a cultural phenomenon that would influence societies around the world. Each culture has woven me into its traditions, creating unique customs around my preparation and consumption.

Take, for example, the Japanese tea ceremony, or chanoyu, where the art of tea becomes a meditative practice. Every movement is intentional, reflecting deep respect for me and the moment. The saying, "一碗の中に世界を探す" (Ichimai no naka ni sekai o sagasu), meaning "to find the world in a single bowl," perfectly captures the essence of this practice. It highlights how a simple bowl of tea can encapsulate the beauty and tranquility of the world.

In stark contrast, the vibrant Indian chai culture thrives on community and warmth, with tea stalls buzzing with life as fze in my rich and diverse heritage. The modern twist on tea consumption, like the Taiwanese bubble tea phenomenon, has captivated younger generations, combining my traditional essence with fun, chewy tapioca pearls, proving that I continue to innovate and inspire.

The health benefits I offer further add to my universal appeal. Rich in antioxidants, vitamins, and minerals, I am celebrated for my ability to boost the immune system, improve digestion, and reduce stress. From the soothing properties of chamomile to the invigorating effects of green tea, there is a version of me for every need and occasion, promoting wellness and balance in our lives.

As you savor each sip, remember that I am more than just a beverage. I am a bridge between cultures, a symbol of hospitality, and a testament to the enduring human spirit. My story is your story, a tale of connection, tradition, and the timeless joy of tea. In the coming chapters, we will delve deeper into the unique tea customs of these countries, exploring the intricate ceremonies and rich traditions that make each tea culture so special.

The Spiritual Side of Me.

As we delve deeper into my world, you'll find that my significance extends beyond mere consumption. I have long been intertwined with spiritual practices and philosophies, serving as a vessel for mindfulness and inner reflection. I invite you to slow down, savor each moment, and connect with something greater than yourself.

In Japan, the tea ceremony embodies Zen principles, where every aspect of my preparation and presentation encourages mindfulness and harmony. Participants engage in a ritual that transcends the act of drinking me, transforming it into a meditative experience that fosters peace and contemplation. As the great tea master Sen no Rikyū once said, "茶道における至高の美は、自然との調和にある" (Chadō ni okeru shikō no bi wa, shizen to no chōwa ni aru), meaning "The highest beauty in the way of tea lies in harmony with nature."

My spiritual journey also includes the tale of Bodhidharma, a monk from India who traveled to China and founded Zen Buddhism. According to legend, Bodhidharma once fell asleep during a nine-year meditation. When he awoke, frustrated with his lack of discipline, he tore off his eyelids and cast them aside. From the ground where they landed, I, a tea plant, sprouted. My leaves, when brewed, helped keep monks awake and focused during long meditations. This story symbolizes my deep connection with Zen Buddhism and the discipline of meditation.

In the realms of Taoism, I symbolize the pursuit of balance and naturalness. The simple act of brewing and enjoying me becomes a pathway to align oneself with the rhythms of nature, reinforcing the idea that tranquility can be found in simplicity. Laozi, the legendary Taoist sage, is often depicted enjoying me in quiet contemplation, reflecting the deep connection between tea and the Taoist philosophy of finding harmony in the natural flow of life.

In India, my spiritual connection is evident through Ayurvedic practices, where various herbal blends support both physical health and spiritual well-being. Each cup of me is more than just a drink; it's an elixir that nurtures the mind, body, and spirit, connecting individuals to their cultural roots and personal journeys. The Sanskrit phrase "आयुर्वेदः च विष्णुः" (Āyurvedaḥ ca viṣṇuḥ), meaning "Ayurveda and Vishnu (the preserver)," underscores the sacredness of Ayurvedic practices, where tea plays a pivotal role.

Image-1.1: Lord Dhanvantari God of Ayurveda

In many monastic traditions, I have played a crucial role in supporting spiritual practice. Buddhist monks in China and Japan have long relied on me to sustain their meditation practices. My gentle stimulant properties help monks remain alert and focused during long periods of meditation, while the ritual of preparing and drinking me fosters a sense of discipline and mindfulness.

Incorporating me into a daily mindfulness routine can help you reconnect with yourself and the present moment. I offer a gentle reminder to pause, breathe, and appreciate the small, often overlooked pleasures that bring richness to our lives.

1.2 - TEA TAXONOMIES

THE CAMELLIA SINENSIS FAMILY

et me take you on a journey through my family tree, my each branch tells a unique story, enriching your appreciation of the beloved beverage we call tea. I am but one leaf of the vast and intricate Camellia sinensis family, and knowing our taxonomy unveils the intricate relationships within the tea world.

The Camellia Sinensis Family.

At the heart of all true teas lies the Camellia sinensis plant, which branches into two primary varieties: Camellia sinensis var. sinensis and Camellia sinensis var. assamica. These varieties are like the siblings in our family, each with distinct characteristics shaped by climate, soil, and processing methods.

Camellia sinensis var. sinensis, originating from China, is known for its delicate flavors and is primarily used for green and white teas. My leaves, when part of this variety, are small and tender, producing subtle and refined tastes that delight the palate.

On the other hand, Camellia sinensis var. assamica, native to India, boasts larger, bolder leaves, perfect for creating robust black teas. When I belong to this variety, my flavors are full-bodied and rich, offering a strong and invigorating experience. Remarkably, once a tea bush matures, it can yield tea for fifty years or more, ensuring a long-lasting supply of this cherished beverage.

Image 1.2 ~ Camellia Sinensis Plant a. Flower b Leaf c. Cross Section

Six Elementary Tea Types:

Within our Camellia family, tea is traditionally categorized into six elementary types, each distinguished by processing methods, oxidation levels, and regions where they are grown. These categories are like the different roles we play, each with unique flavors, aromas, and appearances.

Black Tea: Known for its robust and bold flavor, black tea undergoes full oxidation, which gives it a dark color and rich taste. Varieties like Assam, Darjeeling, and Ceylon fall under this category. When I transform into black tea, my leaves become a deep, dark hue, releasing a powerful and satisfying flavor.

Green Tea: Unoxidized and celebrated for its fresh, grassy, and vegetal taste, green tea is a staple in many cultures, particularly in China and Japan. Popular varieties include Sencha, Longjing, and Matcha. In my green tea form, I retain my natural color and deliver a clean, refreshing taste.

Pu'er Tea: This fermented tea hails from Yunnan, China, and is known for its earthy and mellow flavor. Pu'er tea is aged, sometimes for several years, enhancing its depth and complexity. As Pu'er, I age gracefully, developing rich, nuanced flavors that tell a story of time and tradition.

Oolong Tea: A semi-oxidized tea, oolong strikes a balance between black and green tea. It offers a wide range of flavors, from floral and fruity to toasty and rich. Famous oolongs include Tieguanyin and Da Hong Pao. In my oolong form, I dance between worlds, offering a diverse palate of experiences.

Yellow Tea: Rare and slightly oxidized, yellow tea is similar to green tea but undergoes an additional step called "menhuang," or "sealing yellow," which gives it a mellower flavor and yellow hue. As yellow tea, I offer a gentle, soothing flavor that is both unique and comforting.

White Tea: The least processed of all tea types, white tea is simply withered and dried. It has a delicate, sweet, and subtle flavor, with Silver Needle and White Peony being well-known examples. In my purest form as white tea, I provide a light, ethereal taste that captures the essence of simplicity.

More Traditional Sipping Teas.

With a legacy spanning centuries, I have been a cherished companion in cultures around the world, offering a rich array of flavors and experiences. From the misty heights of Darjeeling to the sunlit expanses of Ceylon, each region has contributed its own unique essence to my story. Assam tea, with its robust and malty notes, Earl Grey adds a touch of bergamot, and English Breakfast, comforting flavors to start your day. Ceylon Breakfast offers a brisk, lively cup, and China Rose brings a gentle floral hint.

Yet, my story doesn't end with these well-known varieties. I have many more beloved relatives who each bring their own distinctive qualities to the world of tea. Keemun and Lapsang Souchong offer rich, complex flavors, while Lemon and Ping Suey infuse a zesty, refreshing twist. Prince of Wales, Russian, and Russian Caravan teas each add their unique flair, and Yunnan delivers a smooth, mellow taste. These varieties showcase the depth and breadth of my heritage, reflecting the diverse cultures and traditions that celebrate tea.

For a deeper dive into these cherished relatives and their distinct characteristics, please refer to the **table** provided. It offers a comprehensive look at the many traditional sipping teas that contribute to my rich tapestry, each with its own story and flavor profile. Join me on this journey through the fascinating world of traditional teas, where every cup connects you to a piece of history and a moment of serenity.

Tea Name	Taste Profile	Notes of Interest	Origin
Assam	Bold, malty, brisk	Highly stimulating, rich in caffeine	Assam, India
Ceylon	Bright, lively, citrusy	Refreshing and aromatic	Sri Lanka
Ceylon Breakfast	Robust, hearty, brisk	Energizing, ideal for a morning boost	Sri Lanka
China Rose	Floral, sweet, smooth	Delicately perfumed, romantic	China
Darjeeling	Muscatel, floral, fruity	Often called the "Champagne of Teas"	Darjeeling, India
Earl Grey	Citrusy, fragrant, bergamot	Elegant and aromatic	England (flavored with bergamot)
English Breakfast	Strong, rich, malty	Classic and invigorating	Blend (originated in England)
Irish Breakfast	Robust, malty, brisk	Heavier and stronger than English Breakfast	Blend (originated in Ireland)
Jasmine	Floral, sweet, fragrant	Romantic and soothing	China
Keemun	Smoky, fruity, winey	Often referred to as the "Bordeaux of Teas"	Qimen, China
Lapsang Souchong	Smoky, woody, tarry	Unique, with a strong smoky aroma	Fujian, China
Lemon	Citrusy, tangy, refreshing	Bright and lively	Various (flavored with lemon)
Ping Suey	Mild, sweet, vegetal	Soft and calming	China
Prince of Wales	Light, smooth, slightly smoky	Elegant and refined	Blend (originated in England)
Russian Caravan	Smoky, malty, sweet	Complex and rich	Blend (originated in Russia)
Yunnan	Earthy, peppery, rich	Bold and flavorful	Yunnan, China

Table 1.1 : Popular Traditional Sipping Teas other than elementary tea

Rare and Exotic Teas from Around the Globe.

Apart from my well-known family and its varieties, I have a few unique relatives known as Rare and Exotic Teas from Around the Globe. Beyond the familiar varieties, the world of tea is rich with rare and exotic offerings. Let me introduce you to some of these extraordinary teas that reflect specific regional practices and climatic conditions. Exploring these rarities allows tea enthusiasts to embark on a sensory journey that transcends traditional boundaries.

One of my most esteemed cousins is Da Hong Pao, often referred to as the "King of Teas." This rare and highly sought-after oolong tea hails from the Wuyi Mountains in China. The leaves are harvested from ancient tea bushes, and the tea is renowned for its complex, robust flavor with notes of roasted nuts and floral undertones. Imagine the care and tradition that goes into every leaf, creating a tea that is both a heritage and a treasure.

Another illustrious relative is Gyokuro, an exquisite shade-grown Japanese green tea. Gyokuro is known for its rich umami flavor and vibrant green color, making it a prized tea for connoisseurs. The process of growing Gyokuro involves shielding the tea plants from direct sunlight for several weeks before harvest, allowing the leaves to develop a deeper, more nuanced flavor. It's a labor of love that results in a truly remarkable tea.

These rare and exotic teas offer a glimpse into the diverse and intricate world of tea. They embody the unique qualities of their regions and the dedication of those who cultivate them. So, as you sip these extraordinary brews, know that you are experiencing something truly special, a testament to the art and tradition of tea-making that has been perfected over centuries.

Wild Teas: Nature's Untouched Brews

Beyond my well-known family and its varieties, I have some wild and untamed relatives known as Wild Teas: Nature's Untouched Brews. These special teas grow freely in their natural habitats, untroubled by human hands. They thrive in remote and ancient landscapes, embodying the very essence of their environment.

In the secluded forests of Yunnan, China, you'll find my wild cousins—ancient tea trees that have stood for hundreds of years. The leaves from these venerable trees are carefully hand-harvested to create unique and flavorful teas. For example, the famed Yunnan Wild Ancient Tree Pu-erh boasts an earthy, rich flavor, thanks to its growth in the deep, untouched forests of Yunnan. This tea is celebrated not just for its complex taste but also for its health benefits, including its ability to aid digestion and lower cholesterol.

Another remarkable member of my wild family is the Liu Bao Tea from Guangxi, China. Often harvested from wild tea bushes in the lush, mountainous regions, Liu Bao Tea is known for its robust, earthy flavor and deep, dark color.

This tea undergoes a unique fermentation process, which imparts a distinctive, mellow taste and complex aroma.

In Taiwan, there are wild teas like the Taiwanese Wild Mountain Oolong, which grows in the high, misty mountains. This tea, with its vibrant floral notes and smooth texture, captures the essence of the high-altitude environment where it thrives. The wild conditions contribute to its unique flavor profile, setting it apart from cultivated teas.

In the dense, untouched jungles of Assam, India, you might come across Assam Wild Black Tea. Grown in remote, wild tea gardens, this tea offers a bold, robust flavor with hints of spice and a deep, malty richness. Its flavor reflects the rugged beauty of its natural habitat, making each cup a true taste of the wild.

Each sip of these wild teas is like tasting a piece of untouched wilderness, a true connection to the earth's ancient and unspoiled beauty. Drinking these brews is not just about enjoying tea but savoring a profound link to nature, in its most authentic and raw form.

Beyond True Teas: The World of Tisanes

While I come from the Camellia family, there's a whole extended family of tisanes that enrich the world of tea with their diverse flavors and benefits. Unlike true teas, which hail from my own Camellia sinensis lineage, tisanes are crafted from a variety of leaves, flowers, herbs, spices, and roots that come from plants other than myself. Think of these as my fascinating cousins, each bringing their own unique qualities and charm to the table.

From the soothing notes of chamomile flowers to the vibrant zest of hibiscus, and the invigorating blend of peppermint, tisanes offer a spectrum of flavors and health benefits that transcend traditional tea.

They encompass herbal teas, flower teas, spice teas, and fruit teas—each with its own distinct profile and therapeutic properties. These delightful blends are like a colorful tapestry woven into the broader world of tea, offering a myriad of experiences for those who seek something beyond the usual.

In today's modern world, tisanes are enjoying a well-deserved spotlight. Whether you're flying across continents or savoring a fine dining experience, you'll likely encounter a refined version of these herbal infusions on your journey. From refreshing mint blends served mid-flight to delicate floral tisanes offered in gourmet restaurants, they've become a staple in luxury settings.

The possibilities are truly endless when it comes to tisanes, and with a bit of creativity, the world of mixology offers even more potential. Crafting new combinations of flowers, herbs, and spices opens up exciting avenues for flavor exploration, making each sip a unique experience.

As we move forward, I'll be sharing an array of both classic and inventive tisane recipes. These will include cherished blends as well as creative concoctions that showcase the versatility and richness of tisanes. So, get ready to explore these wonderful extended family members and discover new favorites that will add even more depth to your tea journey. Whether you're a tea connoisseur or someone looking to try something new, the endless possibilities of tisanes are here to excite and inspire.

1.3 - THE ART OF TEA MAKING

BREWING A PERFECT CUP OF TEA

rafting the perfect cup of tea is both an art and a science, deeply rooted in tradition and enhanced by a touch of scientific understanding. In this chapter, I'll guide you through the essentials of water quality, temperature, tea chemistry, and the tools needed to perfect your brew.

Brewing a Perfect Cup of Tea

"Where there's tea, there's hope." - Arthur Wing Pinero

Making a delicious cup of tea is an art, a delicate dance involving me, the tea leaf, and the right amount of water, precise temperature, meticulous timing, and the perfect vessel. In the hands of a true tea aficionado, even the simplest tea can be transformed into a highly satisfying experience. Conversely, incorrect handling can turn even the most expensive tea into a bitter, undrinkable infusion. Let me share the nuances of brewing that perfect cup of tea with you.

Choosing the Right Tea for Your Mood

I have the magical ability to cater to various moods and occasions. Are you feeling sluggish and in need of an energy boost? Reach for my robust black tea or spicy chai relatives. Need to stay productive and focused? A cup of green tea or yerba mate will do the trick. For a burst of creativity, my rich rooibos cousin is your best bet. When stress is overwhelming, my soothing chamomile relative can help you unwind and find your inner peace.

Selection of Quality Water

Ideal water for brewing me should be free of chlorine and other impurities. Distilled water, however, lacks minerals and can result in a flat-tasting tea. The best choice is filtered water with balanced mineral content, often referred to as "soft water." According to a study published in the Journal of Food Science, water with moderate levels of calcium and magnesium enhances my taste, while high levels of these minerals can make me taste bitter and astringent.

Selection and Temperature of Water

The foundation of any good tea is the water you use. Freshly drawn, cold water is always best for preparing me. However, each type of me requires a different water temperature to bring out its best flavor. For instance, my delicate green and white tea forms should be steeped in water that is between 160°F to 185°F (70°C to 85°C).

My oolong relatives, with their complex flavors, do well with water at 185°F to 205°F (85°C to 96°C). For my black and pu-erh tea forms, boiling water at 200°F to 212°F (93°C to 100°C) is ideal. Before infusion, always ensure your water has reached the desired temperature according to the type of me you are preparing.

Research from the International Journal of Tea Science suggests that brewing my green tea forms at too high a temperature can result in a bitter taste due to the excessive extraction of catechins, while brewing my black tea forms at too low a temperature can lead to a weak, insipid infusion.

Brewing Time

Just as with water temperature, different kinds of me require different brewing times to unlock their full potential. Delicate forms, such as green and white, need shorter brewing times, typically between 1 to 3 minutes.

My oolong relatives can be steeped for 3 to 5 minutes, depending on the type. Hearty black teas and earthy, fermented pu-erh teas benefit from longer infusions, usually between 4 to 7 minutes. It's crucial to adhere to these timings to avoid under or over-extraction, which can result in weak or bitter tea, respectively.

Using the Right Teapot or Teacup Material

The material of your teapot or teacup can significantly impact the brewing process and the final taste of me. My forms that require longer infusion times, like black tea or pu-erh tea, benefit from an iron teapot, which retains heat well and ensures a steady, even extraction.

On the other hand, my green and white tea forms need a teapot that stays cooler to prevent over-brewing. For these, a porcelain or glass teapot is ideal as it allows for better temperature control and does not retain heat excessively.

The Ritual of Brewing

Brewing me is more than just a culinary process; it's a ritual that engages all your senses. The sight of my leaves unfurling, the sound of the water pouring, the aroma that fills the air, the warmth of the cup in your hands, and finally, the taste of me—all contribute to a moment of mindfulness and tranquility.

As you embark on your tea brewing journey, remember that the perfect cup of tea is a personal experience. It's about finding the right balance and combination that suits your palate and mood. Experiment with different types, temperatures, and brewing times to discover your perfect brew.

Tea Type	Ideal Brewing Temperature	Ideal Brewing Time
Black	90-100°C (194-212°F)	3-5 minutes
Green	70-80°C (158-176°F)	2-3 minutes
Pu-er	93°-100°C (200°-212°F)	3-5 minutes
Oolong	80-90°C (176-194°F)	3-5 minutes
Yellow	70°-80°C (160°-180°F)	3-4 minutes
White	75-85°C (167-185°F)	3-5 minutes
Herbal	90-100°C (194-212°F)	5-7 minutes

Table 1.2 : Tea Type, Brewing Temperature & Brewing Time

The Chemistry of Tea and Its Hidden Antioxidants

Unveiling My Secret Ingredients

As a tea leaf, I'm a treasure trove of chemical compounds that contribute to my flavor, aroma, and health benefits. These include polyphenols, amino acids, caffeine, and volatile oils. Let me take you on a journey to understand these components better and see how they shape your tea experience.

Polyphenols: My Powerful Antioxidants

At the heart of my health benefits are polyphenols, particularly catechins in green tea and theaflavins and thearubigins in black tea. These compounds are responsible for my astringency and bitterness, but more importantly, they offer a plethora of health benefits, such as reducing the risk of heart disease and cancer. A review in the American Journal of Clinical Nutrition highlights that regular consumption of tea polyphenols can improve cardiovascular health and reduce oxidative stress.

Amino Acids: The Calming L-Theanine

L-theanine, an amino acid found in me, is known for its calming effects and its ability to enhance cognitive function. Studies have shown that L-theanine can promote relaxation without drowsiness, making me an ideal beverage for both relaxation and focus.

Caffeine: My Gentle Energy Boost

I contain caffeine, a stimulant that can enhance alertness and improve concentration.

The caffeine content varies by my type, with black tea generally containing the most and white tea the least. The presence of L-theanine in me moderates the stimulating effects of caffeine, providing a smoother, more sustained energy boost compared to coffee.

Tools of the Trade: Elevate Your Brewing Experience

Essential Tea Brewing Tools

Using the right tools can significantly impact your tea brewing experience. From precise kettles to quality infusers, the right equipment will help you achieve the perfect brew. Here are some essentials that will guide you in mastering the art of brewing me. Let's elevate your tea-making journey together.

Teapots: Enhancing My Flavor

Traditional teapots, such as Yixing clay pots for oolong tea or porcelain pots for green tea, retain heat well and can enhance the brewing process. The porous nature of Yixing clay absorbs my flavors over time, adding depth to future brews.

Infusers: Unleashing My Full Potential

Stainless steel or silicone infusers are practical for loose leaf tea, allowing me to expand fully and release my flavors. Ensure the infuser has enough space for my leaves to move around for optimal extraction.

Kettles: Precision in Temperature

Electric kettles with temperature control settings are ideal for achieving the precise water temperatures required for different types of me. Brands like Breville and Cuisinart offer kettles with preset temperatures for various teas.

Timers: Perfect Timing

Using a timer ensures that you brew me for the correct duration, preventing over- or under-extraction. The recommended steeping times vary, and adhering to these will help you achieve the perfect cup.

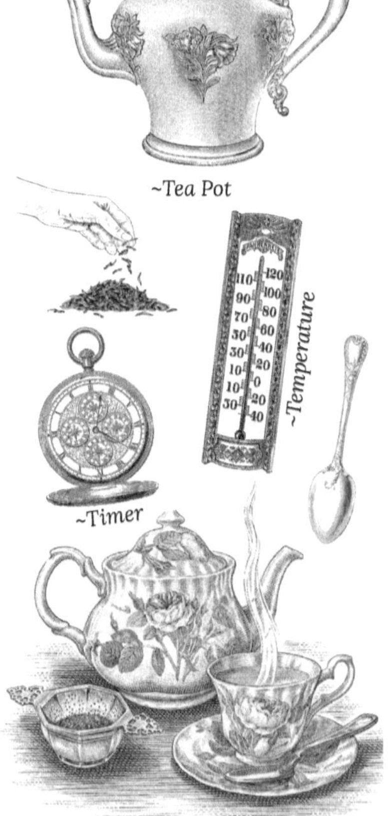

Image 1.3 ~ Essential Tools for perfect tea brewing experience

Mastering the Brew: 7-Step Method to Brewing Excellence

Brewing me to perfection is an art that anyone can master. Below, you will find the process laid out, with tips for tweaking it to suit your own unique taste. Let's embark on this flavorful journey together.

I. Choose Quality Tea: Start with high-quality loose leaf tea, where the flavor and aroma of premium me are far superior to tea bags. Visualize a tea garden, with my leaves glistening in the morning dew, waiting to be carefully picked by skilled hands.

II. Measure the Tea: Use approximately 1 teaspoon of my leaves per 8 ounces of water, adjusting according to personal taste. Imagine a delicate dance, where each teaspoon of my leaves brings a unique performance to your cup.

III. Heat the Water: Use filtered water and heat it to the appropriate temperature for your type of me. Think of the water as my dance partner, perfectly warmed to create the ideal brewing environment.

IV. Preheat the Teapot: Pour a small amount of hot water into the teapot to warm it, then discard the water. Picture the teapot as my cozy home, preheated to welcome me in and make me feel right at home.

V. Infuse the Tea : Place my leaves in the teapot or infuser, pour in the hot water, and cover. Steep for the recommended time. Imagine me unfurling gracefully in the warm water, releasing my flavors and aromas in a delicate embrace.

VI. Strain and Serve: Remove my leaves to prevent over-brewing. Pour the tea into cups and enjoy. Visualize a golden stream of me, filling your cup with warmth and a promise of exquisite taste.

VII. Experiment: Adjust the amount of me, water temperature, and steeping time to find your perfect brew. Think of this step as a creative adventure, where you explore different facets of me to discover your personal favorite.

Troubleshooting Common Brewing Issues

Even seasoned tea enthusiasts encounter challenges in brewing the perfect cup. Here are some common issues and solutions to ensure your tea experience remains delightful.

Bitter Tea: If I taste bitter, it might be due to over-steeping or using water that's too hot. Reduce the steeping time or lower the water temperature.

Weak Tea: If I taste weak, it might be due to under-steeping or using too little tea. Increase the steeping time or the amount of my leaves.

Astringent Tea: If I taste astringent, it might be due to poor water quality. Use filtered or bottled water with balanced minerals.

Experimental Brewing: Exploring New Dimensions

Cold Brew: Smooth and Refreshing

Steep my leaves in cold water for 6-12 hours, allowing ample time for the flavors to infuse gently. This method produces a smooth, less astringent tea with delicate, subtle flavors that are perfect for savoring. Whether you enjoy it plain or with a hint of fruit, cold brew is a delightful way to cool down and relax.

Sparkling Tea: Fizzy and Invigorating

For a bubbly twist, brew a strong tea and mix it with sparkling water to create a fizzy, invigorating beverage. This combination brings a new dimension to your tea experience, making it both refreshing and exciting. Adding a slice of lemon, a few berries, or a sprig of fresh herbs can further enhance the flavor, turning your sparkling tea into a delightful and sophisticated drink.

Tea Cocktails: Sophisticated Sips

Transform your tea into a sophisticated base for cocktails, adding a unique and flavorful twist to your favorite drinks. Mix brewed tea with spirits like gin, vodka, or rum, and complement it with mixers such as tonic water, fruit juice, or even a splash of bitters. Experiment with different combinations to create a variety of tea cocktails that suit your taste and occasion.

Iced Tea: Classic and Cool

Embrace the classic coolness of iced tea by brewing a strong tea, chilling it thoroughly, and serving it over ice. This timeless beverage is both refreshing and versatile, offering endless possibilities for customization. Add a splash of citrus, such as lemon or lime, or garnish with fresh mint leaves to give your iced tea a refreshing twist.

"After guiding you through the art and science of tea brewing, it's time for me, your humble tea leaf, to step back and allow the author to take center stage. I'll be settling in for a delightful pause, eagerly awaiting to see the fresh explorations and creative experiments that lie ahead in the pages of this book."

As you continue on this journey, you'll encounter not just me, but also my intriguing relatives—tisanes and herbal concoctions crafted from flowers, fruits, and a medley of spices and herbs. Each of these diverse brews will offer their own unique charms and stories. So, while I rest for now, keep your senses tuned for the exciting and aromatic discoveries that await. We'll meet again later in the book, ready to share more of the wonders that tea and its kin have to offer.

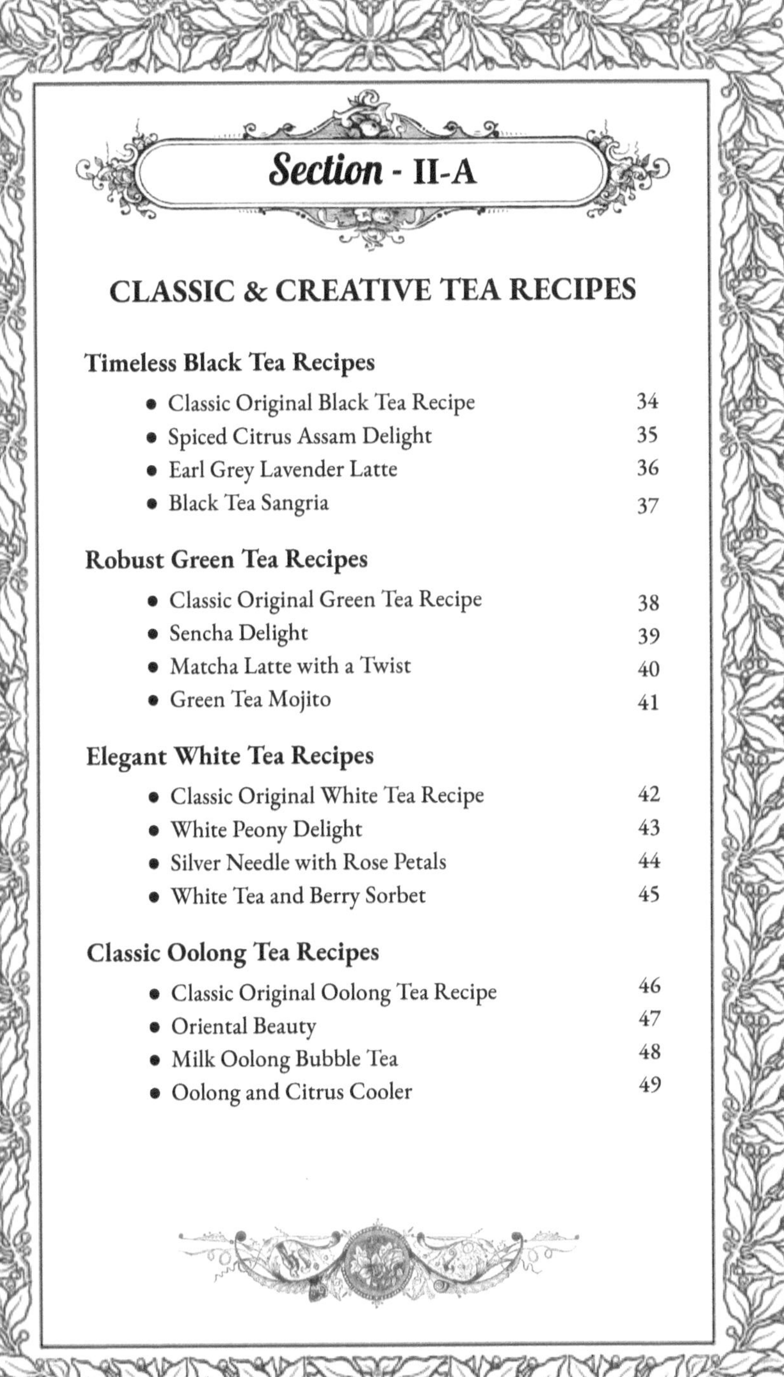

Section - II-A

CLASSIC & CREATIVE TEA RECIPES

"This page is steeping in calm... patience is the secret to a good brew."

1.4 - CLASSIC & CREATIVE TEA RECIPES

ORIGINAL & FUSION RECIPES

n the previous chapters, we delved deep into the fascinating world of tea, exploring the six classic types—Black, Green, Pu-er, Oolong, Yellow, and White. We discussed their origins, unique characteristics, and the traditional ways to enjoy them. But as we journey further, there's even more to uncover.

In the pages ahead, you'll find an array of recipes that celebrate these classic teas in all their glory. Whether you're a purist who enjoys the timeless appeal of traditional brews or an adventurer seeking new flavors, there's something here for everyone. We'll start with the foundational recipes that honor the rich heritage of these teas, offering you a perfect cup just as it has been sipped for centuries.

But why stop there? Beyond the classics, this chapter will guide you through exciting, unique combinations that push the boundaries of tea. Imagine a Black Tea Sangria that refreshes your summer evenings or a Matcha Latte with a modern twist that brightens your mornings. You'll explore ways to infuse your teas with milk, ice, fruits, and spices, creating mocktails and specialty drinks that redefine what a cup of tea can be.

Get ready to transform your tea experience, as we blend tradition with innovation, introducing you to a new spectrum of flavors and possibilities. Whether you're crafting a soothing Silver Needle with Rose Petals or experimenting with bold flavors in a spiced Pu-er, these recipes will open up a world of creative sipping.s

Image 1.4 ~ Tranquil Companionship: Two Men Sharing Tea in Nature's Embrace

Classic Original Black Tea Recipe

Bold | Hearty | Slightly Bitter

About:

Black tea is a fully oxidized tea, known for its robust and hearty flavor. The oxidation process, where the tea leaves are exposed to air, gives black tea its characteristic dark color and rich taste. Originating from various regions, including India, China, and Sri Lanka, black tea is enjoyed for its strong flavor and versatility. It is often the base for many popular blends like Earl Grey and English Breakfast.

Brewing Instructions:

Place 150 ml, or 5 ounces, of water in a kettle and heat it to a rolling boil, between 200° -210°F (93°-99°C). Add 2 to 3 grams, or 1 rounded teaspoon, of loose black tea leaves to a teapot. Pour the hot water over the leaves and steep for 3 to 5 minutes. Strain and serve immediately.

An Extra Special Touch:

Enhance your black tea experience by adding milk, lemon, or a sweetener of your choice. If using milk, add it to the cup first, then pour in the tea to gradually heat the milk. Avoid combining milk and lemon, as this may cause the milk to curdle.

Food Pairing:

Black tea pairs excellently with hearty, rich foods. It complements roast meats such as beef, lamb, and venison, as well as heavy pasta dishes like lasagna. For a sweet pairing, try black tea with dark chocolate or spiced desserts.

Aroma Pairing:

Spices: Cinnamon, clove, cardamom

Citrus: Bergamot (Earl Grey), orange peel

Floral: Rose, lavender

Sweet: Vanilla, caramel

Example Pairings:

An Earl Grey tea with bergamot and a hint of vanilla.

Assam tea with cinnamon and clove.

Image 1.5
~ Bergamot and Orange Peel

Health Benefits:

Black tea contains a significant level of antioxidants, which help prevent DNA damage and slow down the aging process. It is also beneficial for maintaining skin health and may help reduce the risk of skin cancer and supports cardiovascular health .

Black Tea Fusion: Unique Recipes and Combinations

Black tea, with its bold flavors and rich history, holds a special place in the hearts of tea enthusiasts around the world. Unlike its green and white counterparts, black tea undergoes full oxidation, which gives it its characteristic dark color and robust taste. This process also enhances the concentration of caffeine and brings out the complex flavors, making black tea a versatile base for various beverages. From the rolling hills of Assam to the elegant parlors of England, black tea has inspired countless recipes that continue to delight and invigorate.

In this chapter, we explore three robust black tea recipes that showcase the versatility and depth of this beloved beverage: Traditional Assam with a Modern Twist, Earl Grey Lavender Latte, and Black Tea Sangria. Each recipe is crafted to highlight the unique qualities of black tea while offering a contemporary flair that appeals to modern palates.

Spiced Citrus Assam Delight

Assam tea, grown in the northeastern region of India, is known for its strong, malty flavor and bright color. This robust tea is the backbone of many breakfast blends and is often enjoyed with milk and sugar. In this recipe, we give the traditional Assam tea a modern twist by adding spices and a hint of citrus, creating a flavorful and invigorating beverage.

Ingredients:

1 teaspoon of Assam black tea leaves

8 ounces of filtered water

1 cinnamon stick

2-3 cardamom pods

1 slice of fresh ginger & orange

1-2 teaspoons of honey or sugar (optional)

Milk (optional)

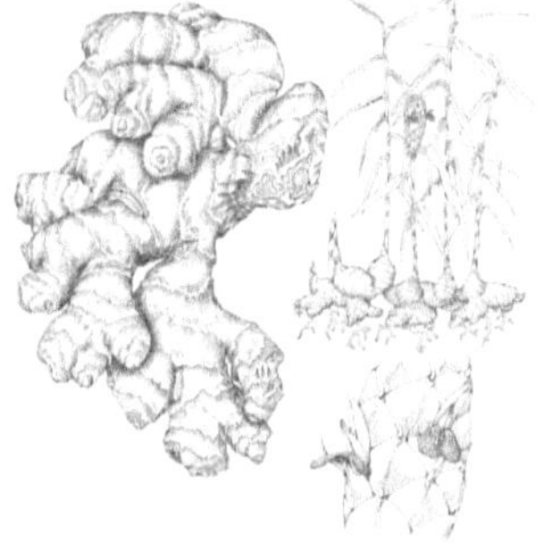

Image 1.6
~ Ginger root and Orange

Instructions:

Boil the Water: Bring the filtered water to a rolling boil (around 100°C or 212°F).

Add Spices: In a teapot or saucepan, add the cinnamon stick, cardamom pods, and ginger slice. Pour the boiling water over the spices and let them steep for 1-2 minutes.

Add Tea Leaves: Add the Assam tea leaves to the spiced water and steep for 3-5 minutes.

Strain and Serve: Strain the tea into a cup, adding the orange slice. Sweeten with honey or sugar if desired. For a creamier texture, add a splash of milk.

Health Benefits:

Assam tea is rich in antioxidants like theaflavins and thearubigins, which can help improve heart health and reduce the risk of chronic diseases.

Interesting Fact:

Assam tea is one of the world's largest tea-producing regions, known for its distinctive malty flavor and strong body. It is often used in traditional Indian chai recipes.

Earl Grey Lavender Latte Recipe

Earl Grey tea, a fragrant blend of black tea and bergamot oil, has been a favorite in British tea culture for centuries. The addition of lavender to this classic tea creates a soothing and aromatic latte that is perfect for relaxing moments.

Ingredients:

1 teaspoon of Earl Grey tea leaves

8 ounces of filtered water

1/2 teaspoon of dried lavender buds

6 ounces of milk (dairy or plant-based)

1-2 teaspoons of honey or vanilla syrup (optional)

Image 1.7
~ *Lavender flower and buds*

Instructions:

Boil the Water: Bring the filtered water to a boil (around 100°C or 212°F).

Steep the Tea and Lavender: In a teapot, add the Earl Grey tea leaves and dried lavender buds. Pour the boiling water over the mixture and steep for 3-5 minutes. Strain the tea into a cup, discarding the leaves and lavender.

Heat and Froth the Milk: In a small saucepan, heat the milk until hot but not boiling. Use a milk frother or whisk to create a frothy texture. Pour the hot, frothy milk into the tea. Sweeten with honey or vanilla syrup if desired.

Health Benefits:

Earl Grey tea contains antioxidants that can help protect against heart disease and cancer. Bergamot oil, a key ingredient in Earl Grey, has been shown to have mood-enhancing properties.

Interesting Fact:

Earl Grey tea was named after Charles Grey, the 2nd Earl Grey and British Prime Minister in the 1830s.

Black Tea Sangria Recipe

Combining the bold flavors of black tea with the refreshing elements of a traditional sangria, Black Tea Sangria is a delightful beverage perfect for social gatherings and hot summer days. This non-alcoholic version is brimming with fruits and subtle sweetness, offering a sophisticated alternative to regular iced tea.

Ingredients:

2 teaspoons of black tea leaves (Darjeeling or Ceylon work well)

16 ounces of filtered water

1 orange & lemon thinly sliced & 1 apple, cored and thinly sliced

1 cup of mixed berries (strawberries, blueberries, raspberries)

2 tablespoons of honey or agave syrup

16 ounces of sparkling water or club soda

Ice cubes & Fresh mint leaves for garnish

Image 1.8
~ Various type of berries

Instructions:

Brew the Tea: Bring the filtered water to a boil and steep the black tea leaves for 3-5 minutes. Strain the tea and let it cool to room temperature. Meanwhile prepare the fruits.

Prepare the Fruit: In a large pitcher, combine the sliced orange, lemon, apple, and mixed berries.

Mix the Tea: Add the cooled black tea to the pitcher. Stir in the honey or agave syrup until dissolved.

Chill: Refrigerate the mixture for at least 1-2 hours before serving to allow the flavors to meld.

Serve: Just before serving, add ice cubes and top off with sparkling water or club soda. Garnish with fresh mint leaves.

Health Benefits:

Black tea is rich in flavonoids, which can help improve heart health and reduce the risk of stroke. The addition of fresh fruits provides vitamins and antioxidants, making this a refreshing and health-conscious beverage.

Interesting Fact:

Sangria, traditionally a Spanish and Portuguese beverage, dates back to the 18th century. By incorporating black tea, this version adds a unique twist while maintaining the essence of the classic sangria.

Classic Original Green Tea Recipe

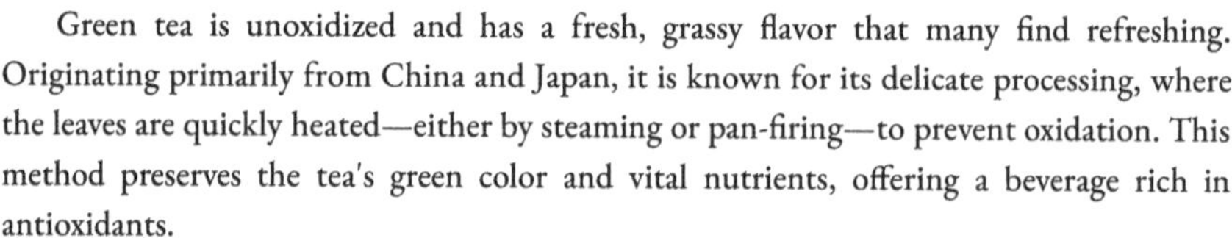

Fresh | Grassy | Slightly Sweet

About:

Green tea is unoxidized and has a fresh, grassy flavor that many find refreshing. Originating primarily from China and Japan, it is known for its delicate processing, where the leaves are quickly heated—either by steaming or pan-firing—to prevent oxidation. This method preserves the tea's green color and vital nutrients, offering a beverage rich in antioxidants.

Brewing Instructions:

Place 150 ml, or 5 ounces, of water in a kettle and heat it to just below boiling, around 170°-185°F (75°-85°C). Add 2 grams, or 1 teaspoon, of loose green tea leaves to a teapot. Pour the water over the tea leaves and steep for 1 to 2 minutes. Avoid overstepping to prevent bitterness. Strain and serve.

An Extra Special Touch:

For a traditional Japanese experience, whisk matcha powder with a bamboo whisk in a bowl until frothy. Add a slice of lemon or a touch of honey for a modern twist. Green tea pairs beautifully with fresh mint leaves for added aroma.

Food Pairing:

Green tea's subtle flavors complement light dishes such as salads, sushi, steamed fish, and soft cheeses. It also pairs well with fresh fruits like berries and citrus.

Aroma Pairing:

Herbs: Mint, lemongrass, basil

Floral: Jasmine, lotus

Fruity: Apple, peach, lemon

Vegetal: Cucumber, fresh grass

Example Pairings:

Jasmine green tea with a touch of lemongrass.

Sencha with mint and a slice of cucumber.

Health Benefits:

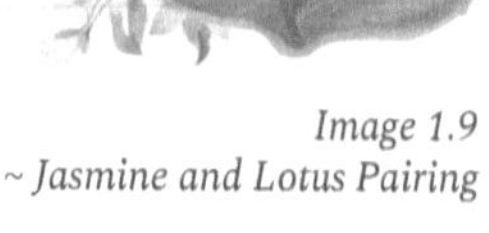

Image 1.9
~ Jasmine and Lotus Pairing

Green tea is renowned for its high concentration of antioxidants, particularly catechins, which help combat inflammation and promote heart health. It also aids in weight management, boosts metabolism, and supports brain function due to its caffeine and L-theanine content.

Green Tea Fusion: Unique Recipes and Combinations

Green tea, revered for its delicate flavors and myriad health benefits, has a timeless appeal that transcends cultures and generations. Originating from the Camellia sinensis plant, green tea undergoes minimal oxidation, preserving its vibrant color and rich array of antioxidants. From the traditional brews of Japan to modern-day culinary innovations, green tea continues to inspire and delight tea enthusiasts worldwide.

The versatility of green tea allows it to be enjoyed in various forms—hot, iced, as a base for creative beverages, or even as an ingredient in culinary dishes. Each method of preparation offers a unique experience, allowing the natural flavors and benefits of green tea to shine through. In this chapter, we explore three timeless green tea recipes that capture the essence of this beloved beverage: Classic Sencha, Matcha Latte with a Twist, and Green Tea Mojito.

Classic Sencha Tea Recipe:

Sencha is the most popular type of green tea in Japan, known for its refreshing taste and vibrant green color. It is harvested from the first and second flushes of the tea plant, making it rich in flavor and nutrients.

Ingredients:

1 teaspoon of sencha green tea leaves

8 ounces of filtered water

Optional: lemon slice or honey for sweetness

Instructions:

Heat the Water: Bring the filtered water to a temperature of 70-80°C (158-176°F). Avoid boiling water as it can scorch the delicate tea leaves and produce a bitter taste.

Preheat the Teapot: Pour a small amount of hot water into the teapot, swirl it around, and discard. This step ensures the teapot is warm and ready for brewing.

Add the Tea Leaves: Place 1 teaspoon of sencha tea leaves into the teapot.

Pour the Water: Gently pour the hot water over the tea leaves.

Steep, Strain and Serve:: Allow the tea to steep for 1-2 minutes. Sencha requires a short steeping time to avoid bitterness. Strain the tea into a cup and enjoy. Add a slice of lemon or a drizzle of honey if desired.

Health Benefits:

Sencha is rich in antioxidants, particularly catechins, which help fight free radicals and reduce inflammation. Regular consumption of sencha can improve cardiovascular health, boost metabolism, and support overall well-being.

Interesting Fact:

Sencha accounts for nearly 80% of the tea produced in Japan and is typically enjoyed multiple times a day by tea connoisseurs for its balanced, refreshing flavor.

Matcha Latte Recipe with a Twist

Matcha, a finely ground powdered green tea, has a long history in Japanese tea ceremonies and has recently gained popularity worldwide for its vibrant color and health benefits. The unique preparation of matcha involves whisking the powder with water, creating a frothy, rich tea.

Ingredients:

1 teaspoon of matcha powder

2 ounces of hot water (not boiling, around 80°C/176°F)

6 ounces of milk (dairy or plant-based)

1 tablespoon of honey or maple syrup (optional)

A pinch of cinnamon or nutmeg for a twist

Instructions:

Prepare the Matcha: Sift 1 teaspoon of matcha powder into a bowl to remove any clumps.

Add Hot Water: Pour 2 ounces of hot water with suggested temorature, slowely over the matcha powder.

Whisk: Using a bamboo whisk (chasen) or a small hand whisk, whisk the matcha in a zigzag motion until it becomes frothy.

Heat the Milk: In a small saucepan, heat the milk until it's hot but not boiling. Froth the milk using a milk frother or whisk.

Combine: Pour the frothy matcha into a cup, then add the hot, frothed milk. Stir to combine.

Sweeten and Spice: Add honey or maple syrup to taste and a pinch of cinnamon or nutmeg for an extra twist.

Health Benefits:

Matcha is a powerhouse of antioxidants, including EGCG (epigallocatechin gallate), which has been shown to boost metabolism and aid in weight loss.

It also provides a calm, focused energy due to the combination of caffeine and L-theanine.

Interesting Fact:

One cup of matcha is equivalent to consuming the nutrients from 10 cups of regularly brewed green tea, making it a potent source of vitamins, minerals, and antioxidants.

Green Tea Mojito Recipe:

Combining the refreshing qualities of green tea with the zesty, invigorating flavors of a classic mojito, the Green Tea Mojito is a delightful twist on a popular cocktail. This non-alcoholic version is perfect for a sunny afternoon or as a healthy party beverage.

Ingredients:

1 teaspoon of loose leaf green tea (or 1 green tea bag)

8 ounces of filtered water

1 tablespoon of honey or agave syrup

1 lime, cut into wedges

10 fresh mint leaves

Sparkling water or club soda

Ice cubes

Instructions:

Brew the Tea: Heat the filtered water to 80-85°C (176-185°F). Steep the green tea for 2-3 minutes, then strain and let it cool to room temperature.

Prepare the Mojito Base: In a glass, muddle the mint leaves and lime wedges together to release their flavors. Add the honey or agave syrup and mix well.

Combine: Fill the glass with ice cubes. Pour the cooled green tea over the ice and stir.

Top Up: Add sparkling water or club soda to fill the glass. Give it a gentle stir.

Garnish: Garnish with extra mint leaves and a lime wedge.

Health Benefits:

This refreshing drink combines the antioxidant properties of green tea with the digestive benefits of mint and the vitamin C boost from lime. It's a hydrating and revitalizing beverage perfect for hot days.

Interesting Fact:

Green tea contains catechins that help enhance the body's ability to burn fat, making this mojito not only a tasty treat but also a health-conscious choice.

Classic Original White Tea Recipe

Delicate | Floral | Lightly Sweet

About:

White tea is the least processed of all teas, made from young leaves and buds that are simply withered and dried. Originating from the Fujian province of China, it is known for its subtle, sweet flavor and pale color. White tea's minimal processing ensures it retains a high amount of antioxidants, making it both a delicate and healthful choice.

Brewing Instructions:

Place 150 ml, or 5 ounces, of water in a kettle and heat it to around 160°-180°F (70°-80° C). Add 2 grams, or 1 teaspoon, of loose white tea leaves to a teapot. Pour the water over the tea leaves and steep for 4 to 5 minutes. Strain and serve.

An Extra Special Touch:

For an enhanced experience, infuse white tea with a few dried rose petals or lavender buds. A hint of honey can add a touch of sweetness without overpowering the delicate flavor.

Food Pairing:

White tea pairs well with light foods such as soft cheeses, melon, cucumber sandwiches, and mild seafood dishes like scallops. It also complements delicate desserts like macarons and sponge cakes.

Aroma Pairing:

Floral: Rose, lavender, elderflower

Fruity: Pear, melon, lychee

Herbs: Chamomile, thyme

Sweet: Honey, vanilla

Example Pairings:

White Peony tea with rose petals and a hint of honey.

Silver Needle with elderflower and pear.

Health Benefits:

White tea boasts a high level of antioxidants, particularly polyphenols, which can protect the skin from damage and promote overall health.

It has been linked to improved cardiovascular health, reduced inflammation, and enhanced weight loss efforts.

White Tea Fusion: Unique Recipes and Combinations

White tea, the most delicate and minimally processed of all teas, captures the pure essence of the Camellia sinensis plant. Harvested primarily in the Fujian province of China, white tea is made from the young leaves and unopened buds of the tea plant, which are simply withered and dried. This gentle processing preserves the tea's natural flavors and high concentration of antioxidants, making it a prized choice for tea connoisseurs seeking a light, elegant brew.

In this chapter, we delve into the world of white tea with three exquisite recipes: White Peony Delight, Silver Needle with Rose Petals, and White Tea and Berry Sorbet. Each recipe showcases the subtlety and sophistication of white tea, offering a unique and refreshing experience.

White Peony Delight Recipe

White Peony, or Bai Mudan, is a beloved variety of white tea known for its fuller flavor compared to the more delicate Silver Needle. It includes both young leaves and buds, giving it a richer taste while maintaining the lightness characteristic of white tea.

Ingredients:

1 teaspoon of White Peony (Bai Mudan) tea leaves

8 ounces of filtered water

Optional: honey or lemon for additional flavor

Instructions:

Heat the Water: Bring the filtered water to a temperature of 75-85°C (167-185°F). Avoid boiling water as it can scorch the delicate leaves.

Preheat the Teapot: Pour a small amount of hot water into the teapot, swirl it around, and discard. This warms the teapot and prepares it for brewing.

Add the Tea Leaves: Place 1 teaspoon of White Peony tea leaves into the teapot.

Pour the Water: Gently pour the hot water over the tea leaves.

Steep: Allow the tea to steep for 3-5 minutes. White Peony tea can handle a slightly longer steep time compared to other white teas without becoming bitter.

Strain and Serve: Strain the tea into a cup. Add honey or lemon if desired for a touch of sweetness or zest.

Health Benefits:

White Peony tea is rich in polyphenols, which are known for their antioxidant properties. These compounds help combat free radicals, reduce inflammation, and support cardiovascular health. The tea also has a mild caffeine content, providing a gentle energy boost without the jitters.

Interesting Fact:

White Peony tea gets its name from the appearance of its dried leaves, which resemble peony flowers. It is traditionally enjoyed in the spring, following the first harvest.

Silver Needle with Rose Petals Recipe

Silver Needle, or Bai Hao Yinzhen, is the most revered and highest grade of white tea. Made exclusively from the young buds of the tea plant, Silver Needle has a light, sweet, and floral flavor. Adding rose petals enhances its delicate aroma, creating a luxurious and aromatic tea experience.

Ingredients:

1 teaspoon of Silver Needle (Bai Hao Yinzhen) tea buds

8 ounces of filtered water

1 teaspoon of dried rose petals

Optional: honey or a few drops of rose water for additional flavor

Instructions:

Heat the Water: Bring the filtered water to a temperature of 75-80°C (167-176°F).

Preheat the Teapot: Warm the teapot with hot water and discard.

Add the Tea and Rose Petals: Place 1 teaspoon of Silver Needle tea buds and 1 teaspoon of dried rose petals into the teapot.

Pour the Water: Gently pour the hot water over the tea and rose petals.

Steep: Allow the tea to steep for 2-4 minutes.

Strain and Serve: Strain the tea into a cup. Sweeten with honey or add a few drops of rose water if desired.

Health Benefits:

Silver Needle tea is packed with catechins, a type of antioxidant that helps protect cells from damage. It also has anti-inflammatory properties and can support skin health. The addition of rose petals provides extra vitamin C and enhances relaxation.

Interesting Fact:

Silver Needle tea was once reserved exclusively for the Chinese Imperial family due to its rarity and labor-intensive production process. It remains one of the most sought-after and expensive teas in the world.

White Tea and Berry Sorbet Recipe

For a refreshing and healthy dessert, this White Tea and Berry Sorbet combines the light, floral notes of white tea with the natural sweetness and tartness of berries. This sorbet is a perfect treat for warm days or as a palate cleanser between meals.

Ingredients:

2 teaspoons of white tea leaves (White Peony or Silver Needle)

2 cups of filtered water

1 cup of mixed berries (strawberries, blueberries, raspberries)

1/2 cup of sugar or honey

1 tablespoon of lemon juice

Instructions:

Brew the Tea: Heat the filtered water to 75-85°C (167-185°F) and steep the white tea leaves for 4-5 minutes. Strain the tea and let it cool to room temperature.

Prepare the Berries: In a blender, combine the mixed berries, sugar or honey, and lemon juice. Blend until smooth.

Mix the Tea and Berries: Pour the cooled tea into the berry mixture and blend until well combined.

Freeze the Mixture: Pour the mixture into a shallow dish or ice cream maker. If using a shallow dish, freeze for 1-2 hours, stirring every 30 minutes to break up ice crystals, until the sorbet is firm.

Serve: Scoop the sorbet into bowls or glasses and enjoy. Garnish with fresh berries or mint leaves if desired.

Health Benefits:

This sorbet is a guilt-free dessert packed with antioxidants from both the white tea and berries. The vitamins and minerals in the berries support immune function and skin health, while the low sugar content makes it a healthier alternative to traditional ice cream.

Interesting Fact:

White tea's high antioxidant levels make it an excellent addition to any diet focused on anti-aging and overall wellness. Combining it with berries, which are also rich in antioxidants, creates a powerful duo for health benefits.

Classic Original Oolong Tea Recipe

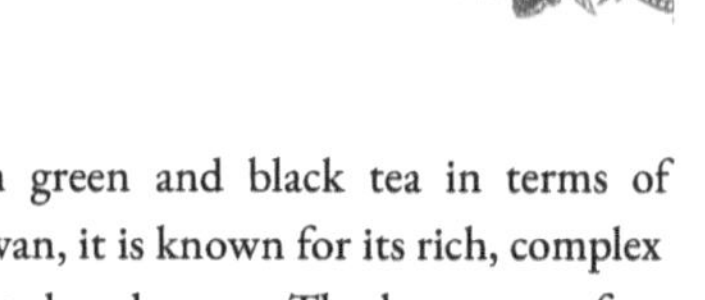

Complex | Floral | Smooth

About:

Oolong tea is semi-oxidized, placing it between green and black tea in terms of oxidation and flavor. Originating from China and Taiwan, it is known for its rich, complex taste, which can range from floral and fruity to roasted and nutty. The leaves are often rolled, curled, or twisted, and can be infused multiple times, with each infusion offering a different flavor profile.

Brewing Instructions:

Place 150 ml, or 5 ounces, of water in a kettle and heat it to around 185°-205°F (85°-96° C). Add 2 grams, or 1 teaspoon, of loose oolong tea leaves to a teapot. Pour the water over the tea leaves and steep for 3 to 5 minutes. Strain and serve. The leaves can be re-steeped multiple times.

An Extra Special Touch:

Try adding a slice of dried orange or a few jasmine flowers for a fragrant twist. Oolong tea is also excellent cold-brewed, which brings out its natural sweetness and complexity.

Food Pairing:

Oolong tea pairs well with a variety of foods, including seafood, poultry, and dim sum. It also complements creamy desserts like panna cotta and fruit-based sweets.

Aroma Pairing:

Floral: Orchid, osmanthus, magnolia

Fruity: Peach, apricot, citrus

Nutty: Almond, chestnut

Spicy: Ginger, star anise

Example Pairings:

Oriental Beauty oolong with osmanthus flowers.

Milk oolong with a touch of almond and peach.

Health Benefits:

Oolong tea offers a unique blend of antioxidants found in both green and black teas, aiding in weight management and improving metabolism. It supports heart health, reduces stress levels, and promotes mental alertness.

Oolong Tea Fusion: Unique Recipes and Combinations

Oolong tea, known for its unique and complex flavor profile, occupies a special place in the world of tea. Falling somewhere between green and black tea in terms of oxidation, oolong tea offers a diverse range of tastes and aromas, from floral and fruity to toasty and nutty. This versatility makes it a favorite among tea enthusiasts and an exciting ingredient for a variety of tea recipes.

In this chapter, we explore three delightful oolong tea recipes: Oriental Beauty, Milk Oolong Bubble Tea, and Oolong and Citrus Cooler. Each recipe showcases the distinct characteristics of oolong tea while providing a modern twist that appeals to contemporary tastes.

Oriental Beauty Tea Recipe

Oriental Beauty, also known as Bai Hao oolong, is a highly prized Taiwanese tea with a unique flavor profile. This tea is known for its natural sweetness, floral notes, and honey-like aftertaste, which result from a specific oxidation process and the presence of leafhopper insect bites that enhance the tea's flavor.

Ingredients:

1 teaspoon of Oriental Beauty oolong tea leaves

8 ounces of filtered water : Optional: honey or a few drops of orange blossom water

Instructions:

Heat the Water: Bring the filtered water to a temperature of 85-90°C (185-194°F). Avoid boiling water as it can ruin the delicate flavors.

Preheat the Teapot: Pour a small amount of hot water into the teapot, swirl it around, and discard. This warms the teapot and prepares it for brewing.

Add the Tea Leaves: Place 1 teaspoon of Oriental Beauty oolong tea leaves into the teapot.

Pour the Water: Gently pour the hot water over the tea leaves.

Steep, Strain and Serve: Allow the tea to steep for 2-4 minutes. Taste periodically to ensure it reaches your desired strength. Strain the tea into a cup. Add honey or orange blossom water if desired for an extra touch of sweetness and floral aroma.

Health Benefits:

Oriental Beauty oolong tea is rich in polyphenols and antioxidants, which can help boost metabolism, improve heart health, and provide anti-inflammatory benefits. The unique processing of this tea also enhances its immune-boosting properties.

Interesting Fact:

Oriental Beauty tea was famously named by Queen Elizabeth II after she tasted it and was charmed by its exquisite flavor and appearance. The tea leaves' colorful, white-tipped appearance contributed to its royal endorsement.

Milk Oolong Bubble Tea Recipe

Milk oolong, also known as Jin Xuan, is a creamy and smooth oolong tea from Taiwan. Its natural milky flavor, derived from the specific cultivar and growing conditions, makes it an ideal base for bubble tea—a trendy and delightful beverage loved by many.

Ingredients:

1 teaspoon of Milk Oolong tea leaves

8 ounces of filtered water

1/2 cup of tapioca pearls

1 cup of milk (dairy or plant-based)

1-2 tablespoons of sweetened condensed milk or honey & Ice cubes

Instructions:

Cook the Tapioca Pearls: Follow the package instructions to cook the tapioca pearls. Once cooked, rinse them with cold water and set aside.

Brew the Tea: Bring the filtered water to a temperature of 85-90°C (185-194°F). Steep the Milk Oolong tea leaves for 3-5 minutes, then strain and let the tea cool to room temperature.

Prepare the Milk Tea: In a shaker or mixing glass, combine the brewed Milk Oolong tea, milk, and sweetened condensed milk or honey. Shake or stir until well combined.

Assemble the Bubble Tea: Place the cooked tapioca pearls at the bottom of a glass. Add ice cubes and pour the milk tea mixture over the top.

Serve: Serve with a wide straw and enjoy this creamy, refreshing bubble tea.

Health Benefits:

Milk oolong tea contains antioxidants that can help lower cholesterol, improve digestion, and enhance mental alertness. The tapioca pearls provide a chewy texture and add fun to the drink without significant nutritional benefits.

Interesting Fact:

Milk oolong's creamy flavor is natural and not derived from added milk or dairy products. The unique taste is a result of the specific tea cultivar and processing techniques used by tea growers in Taiwan.

Oolong and Citrus Cooler Recipe

Combining the rich, toasty flavors of oolong tea with the refreshing zest of citrus fruits, this Oolong and Citrus Cooler is a perfect drink for hot summer days. It's a vibrant and revitalizing beverage that highlights the versatility of oolong tea.

Ingredients:

1 teaspoon of oolong tea leaves (Tie Guan Yin or Da Hong Pao work well)

8 ounces of filtered water

1/2 cup of fresh orange juice

1/4 cup of fresh lemon juice

1-2 tablespoons of honey or agave syrup

Ice cubes

Orange and lemon slices and fresh mint leaves for garnish

Instructions:

Brew the Tea: Bring the filtered water to a temperature of 90-95°C (194-203°F). Steep the oolong tea leaves for 3-5 minutes. Strain the tea and let it cool to room temperature.

Mix the Citrus Juices: In a pitcher, combine the fresh orange juice, lemon juice, and honey or agave syrup. Stir until the sweetener is fully dissolved.

Combine and Chill: Add the brewed oolong tea to the citrus mixture. Stir well and refrigerate until chilled.

Serve: Fill glasses with ice cubes and pour the oolong citrus mixture over the ice. Garnish with orange and lemon slices and fresh mint leaves.

Health Benefits:

Oolong tea provides a wealth of antioxidants and polyphenols that support heart health, aid digestion, and help in weight management. The citrus fruits add a dose of vitamin C, enhancing immune function and providing a refreshing flavor.

Interesting Fact:

Oolong tea, with its partially oxidized leaves, is known for its complex and varied flavor profiles, making it a favorite among tea enthusiasts who enjoy exploring different taste sensations.

Tea Typology Challenge
Guess the Tea Type

Across

[4] Delicate, subtle, with natural sweetness and floral notes.
[6] A complex blend of floral and fruity flavors.

Down

[1] Earthy, aged, with a rich, smooth, and fermented taste.
[2] Mellow, sweet, and creamy with a warm, golden color.
[3] Light, grassy, and refreshing with a vibrant green hue.
[5] Bold, rich, and malty with deep amber tones.

Section - II-B

CLASSIC & CREATIVE TEA RECIPES

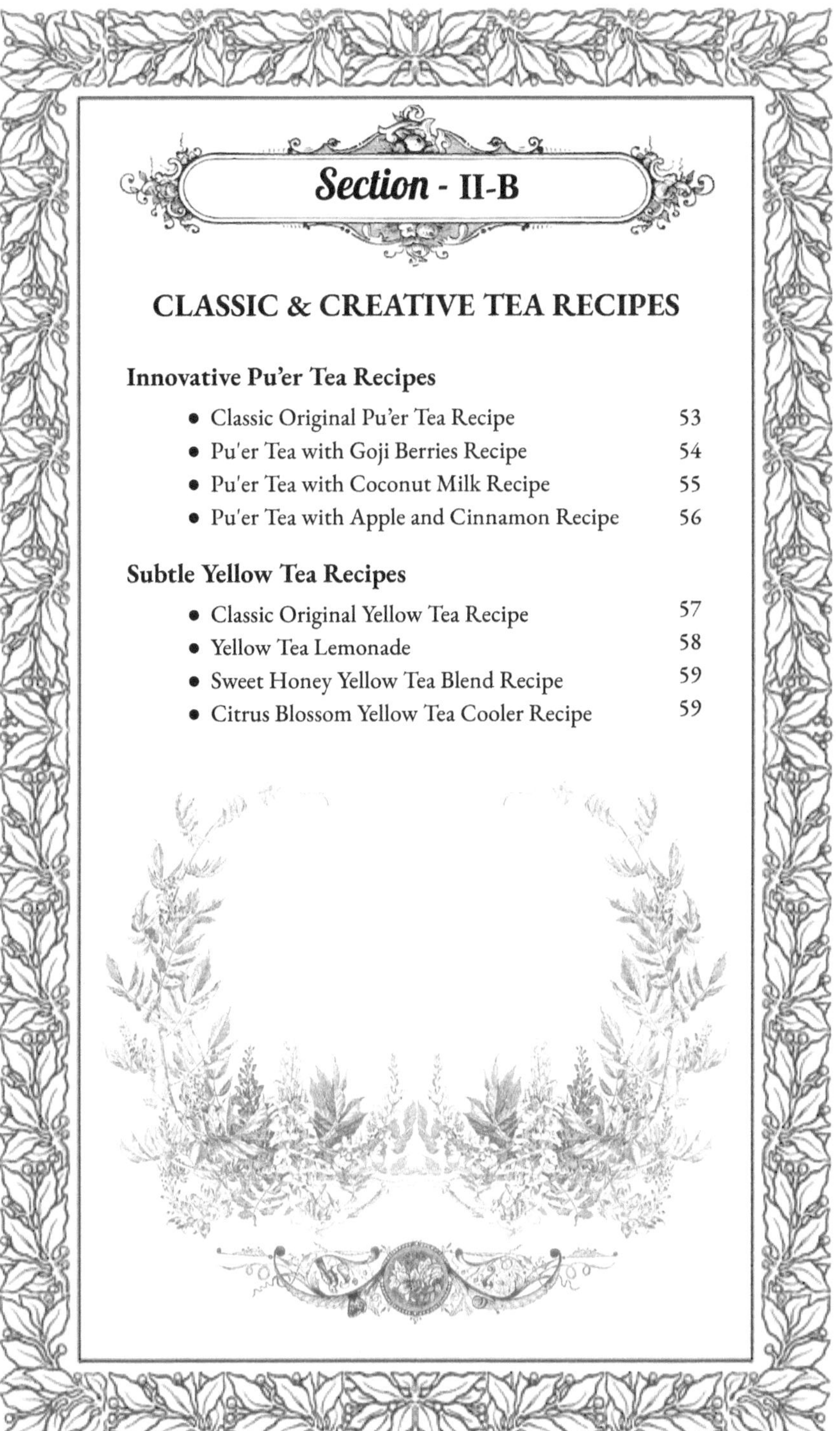

"This page has steeped in quiet, turn the next one to discover the flavor."

Classic Original Pu'er Tea Recipe

Earthy | Mellow | Rich

About:

Pu'er tea is a fermented and aged tea from the Yunnan province of China. It is known for its deep, earthy flavor and unique aging process, which can last for several years, enhancing its complexity. Pu-erh is often compressed into cakes or bricks and can be aged like fine wine.

Brewing Instructions:

Place 150 ml, or 5 ounces, of water in a kettle and heat it to a rolling boil, around 200° -212°F (93°-100°C). Rinse the pu-erh tea leaves with hot water to awaken them. Add 2 to 3 grams, or 1 teaspoon, of rinsed pu-erh tea leaves to a teapot. Pour the hot water over the leaves and steep for 3 to 5 minutes. Strain and serve. The leaves can be re-steeped multiple times.

An Extra Special Touch:

For a richer experience, try adding a slice of ginger or a dash of cinnamon. Pu-erh tea also pairs well with dried fruits like dates and figs.

Food Pairing:

Pu'er tea's robust flavor complements rich, savory foods such as stews, roasted meats, and aged cheeses. It also pairs well with dark chocolate and spiced desserts.

Aroma Pairing:

Earthy: Mushroom, forest floor, wet leaves

Spicy: Cinnamon, anise, ginger

Sweet: Molasses, dark chocolate, caramel

Fruity: Dried dates, figs, plums

Example Pairings:

Aged pu-erh with dried figs and a hint of dark chocolate.

Raw pu-erh with ginger and a touch of molasses.

Health Benefits:

Pu'er tea is known for its probiotic properties, which support gut health. It aids in digestion, helps lower cholesterol levels, and promotes weight loss. The fermentation process also enhances its antioxidant content. Additionally, Pu'er tea is believed to boost cardiovascular health by improving blood circulation and reducing inflammation.

Pu'er Tea Fusion: Unique Recipes and Combinations

Pu'er tea, originating from Yunnan Province in China, is celebrated for its rich, earthy flavor and impressive aging potential. This unique tea undergoes a fermentation process that sets it apart from other teas, resulting in a complex taste profile that matures over time. With notes ranging from woody and mushroom-like to sweet and mellow, pu'er tea offers a sensory experience unlike any other. Its robust character makes it a fascinating addition to various recipes, bringing depth and nuance to both traditional and modern tea concoctions.

In this chapter, we delve into three intriguing pu'er tea recipes: Classic Pu'er Tea, Pu'er Tea Latte, and Spiced Pu'er Tea Punch. Each recipe highlights the distinctive qualities of pu'er tea, showcasing its versatility and ability to harmonize with diverse ingredients.

Pu'er Tea with Goji Berries Recipe

Pu'er Tea with Goji Berries combines the deep, earthy notes of pu'er with the sweet, tangy flavor of goji berries. This blend provides a smooth, tasty, delightful and nourishing tea experience.

Ingredients:

1 teaspoon of pu'er tea leaves

8 ounces of filtered water

1 tablespoon of dried goji berries

Honey to taste

Instructions:

Rinse the Tea Leaves: Place the pu'er tea leaves in a teapot. Pour hot water (around 90° C or 194°F) over the leaves and quickly discard the water.

Heat the Water: Boil the filtered water and let it cool slightly to around 90°C (194°F).

Add the Tea Leaves and Goji Berries: Place the rinsed pu'er tea leaves and dried goji berries into the teapot.

Pour the Water: Gently pour the hot water over the tea leaves and goji berries.

Steep: Allow the tea to steep for 3-5 minutes. Taste periodically to achieve the desired strength.

Strain and Sweeten: Strain the tea into a cup, removing the tea leaves and goji berries. Add honey to taste and stir well.

Serve: Enjoy the Pu'er Tea with Goji Berries hot, appreciating the combination of earthy tea and sweet, tangy berries.

Health Benefits:

Enhances immunity, improves eyesight, and offers antioxidant protection. The combination of pu'er and goji berries supports overall well-being.

Interesting Facts:

Goji berries, also known as wolfberries, have been used in traditional Chinese medicine for centuries and are believed to boost the immune system and improve eyesight

Pu'er Tea with Coconut Milk Recipe

Pu'er Tea with Coconut Milk is a creamy, indulgent drink that blends the boldness of pu'er tea with the smooth, tropical flavor of coconut milk. A unique and satisfying treat.

Ingredients:

1 teaspoon of pu'er tea leaves

8 ounces of filtered water

4 ounces of coconut milk

Sweetener to taste (honey or sugar)

Pinch of cinnamon (optional)

Instructions:

Rinse the Tea Leaves: Place the pu'er tea leaves in a teapot. Pour hot water (around 90° C or 194°F) over the leaves and quickly discard the water.

Heat the Water: Boil the filtered water and let it cool slightly to around 90°C (194°F).

Add the Tea Leaves: Place the rinsed pu'er tea leaves into the teapot.

Pour the Water: Gently pour the hot water over the tea leaves.

Steep: Allow the tea to steep for 3-5 minutes. Taste periodically to achieve the desired strength.

Heat the Coconut Milk: While the tea is steeping, heat the coconut milk in a small saucepan over medium heat until warm.

Combine: Strain the brewed pu'er tea into a cup and add the warm coconut milk.

Sweeten and Spice: Add sweetener as per required taste and a pinch of cinnamon if desired. Stir well.

Serve: Enjoy the Pu'er Tea with Coconut Milk hot, savoring the blend of earthy tea and creamy coconut.

Health Benefits:

Rich in healthy fats from coconut milk, supports heart health, and provides an energy boost. Pu'er tea's antioxidants and digestion aids are enhanced by coconut's nutrients.

Interesting Fact:

Coconut milk adds a rich, creamy texture to tea while being lactose-free, making it a popular choice for those seeking dairy alternatives.

Pu'er Tea with Apple and Cinnamon Recipe

Pu'er Tea with Apple and Cinnamon is a warming blend that combines the earthy richness of Pu'er tea with the sweet, spiced flavors of apple and cinnamon.

Ingredients:

1 teaspoon of pu'er tea leaves

8 ounces of filtered water

1 apple, sliced

1 cinnamon stick and honey to taste

Instructions:

Rinse the Tea Leaves: Place the pu'er tea leaves in a teapot. Pour hot water (around 90° C or 194°F) over the leaves and quickly discard the water.

Heat the Water: Boil the filtered water and let it cool slightly to around 90°C (194°F).

Add the Tea Leaves, Apple Slices, and Cinnamon Stick: Place the rinsed pu'er tea leaves, apple slices, and cinnamon stick into the teapot.

Pour the Water & Steep: Gently pour the hot water over the tea leaves, apple slices, and cinnamon stick. Allow the tea to steep for 3-5 minutes. Taste periodically to achieve the desired strength.

Strain and Sweeten: Strain the tea into a cup, removing the tea leaves, apple slices, and cinnamon stick. Add honey to taste and stir well.

Serve: Enjoy the Pu'er Tea with Apple and Cinnamon hot, appreciating the harmonious blend of earthy tea, sweet apple, and warm cinnamon.

Health Benefits:

Boosts metabolism, regulates blood sugar levels, and provides anti-inflammatory benefits.

Classic Original Yellow Tea Recipe

Mellow | Sweet | Slightly Nutty

About:

Yellow tea is a rare and slightly oxidized tea that undergoes a unique processing step called "menhuang" or "sealing yellow," which gives it its distinct flavor and yellow hue. Originating from China, yellow tea is similar to green tea but has a mellower taste and smoother finish.

Brewing Instructions:

Place 150 ml, or 5 ounces, of water in a kettle and heat it to around 160°-180°F (70°-80° C). Add 2 grams, or 1 teaspoon, of loose yellow tea leaves to a teapot. Pour the water over the tea leaves and steep for 3 to 4 minutes. Strain and serve.

An Extra Special Touch:

Infuse yellow tea with a few slices of pear or a sprinkle of chamomile for a calming effect. A touch of agave syrup can enhance its natural sweetness.

Food Pairing:

Yellow tea pairs well with mild foods such as poached chicken, steamed vegetables, and light salads. It also complements sweet pastries and almond cookies.

Aroma Pairing:

Fruity: Apricot, peach, citrus zest

Floral: Marigold, chrysanthemum

Sweet: Honey, vanilla

Nutty: Hazelnut, almond

Example Pairings:

Junshan Yinzhen yellow tea with marigold and honey.

Meng Ding Huang Ya with a touch of apricot and almond.

Health Benefits:

Yellow tea is rich in antioxidants and supports overall wellness. It helps boost metabolism, improves mental clarity, and promotes a calm, relaxed state.

Interesting Facts:

Yellow tea was once reserved exclusively for Chinese royalty and high-ranking officials due to its rarity and the meticulous craftsmanship required to produce it. This exclusivity earned it the nickname "Imperial Tea".

Yellow Tea Fusion: Unique Recipes and Combinations

Yellow tea, known for its delicate flavor and unique processing, is a rare and treasured variety of tea. Originating from China, yellow tea undergoes a slow fermentation process that imparts a smooth, mellow taste with subtle floral and fruity notes. This nuanced tea offers a refined experience, making it a versatile ingredient for a range of creative recipes. Its golden hue and rich flavor profile lend themselves to both traditional and innovative tea concoctions.

In this chapter, we explore three delightful yellow tea recipes: Junshan Yinzhen Classic, Yellow Tea Lemonade, and Sweet Honey Yellow Tea Blend. Each recipe highlights the distinct qualities of yellow tea, showcasing its versatility and ability to complement diverse flavors.

Yellow Tea Lemonade Recipe

This refreshing blend combines the subtle flavors of yellow tea with the tangy zest of lemonade.

Ingredients:

1 teaspoon of yellow tea leaves

8 ounces of filtered water

2 tablespoons of lemon juice

1 tablespoon of honey

Lemon slices for garnish

Instructions:

Heat the Water: Boil filtered water and let it cool to around 80°C (176°F).

Steep the Tea: Place the yellow tea leaves in a teapot. Pour the cooled water over the leaves.

Infuse: Allow the tea to steep for 2-3 minutes. Strain the tea into a pitcher.

Mix: Add lemon juice and honey to the brewed tea. Stir well to combine.

Serve: Chill the tea in the refrigerator. Serve over ice with lemon slices for a refreshing twist.

Health Benefits:

This lemonade not only provides hydration but also offers antioxidants and vitamin C from the lemon, while the natural sweetness makes it a refreshing and guilt-free treat.

Interesting Facts:

Yellow tea lemonade is a unique and innovative way to enjoy the sophisticated flavors of yellow tea in a chilled, invigorating format.

Sweet Honey Yellow Tea Blend Recipe

This recipe blends the smoothness of yellow tea with the natural sweetness of honey for a comforting and soothing beverage.

Ingredients:

1 teaspoon of yellow tea leaves

8 ounces of filtered water

1-2 tablespoons of honey

Instructions:

Heat the Water: Boil filtered water and let it cool to around 80°C (176°F).

Steep the Tea: Place the yellow tea leaves in a teapot. Pour the cooled water over the leaves.

Infuse: Allow the tea to steep for 2-3 minutes. Strain the tea into a cup.

Sweeten: Stir in honey to taste, ensuring it dissolves completely.

Serve: Enjoy this sweet and soothing yellow tea blend warm or at room temperature.

Health Benefits:

Combining honey with yellow tea enhances its soothing properties and adds a touch of natural sweetness.

Interesting Facts:

Honey has been used as a natural sweetener for centuries and complements the mellow flavor of yellow tea beautifully.

Citrus Blossom Yellow Tea Cooler Recipe

This vibrant recipe blends the subtle richness of yellow tea with the zesty flavors of citrus fruits and a hint of floral elegance.

It's a refreshing and aromatic beverage perfect for warm days or special occasions, and the unique combination of ingredients creates a delicate balance that's both invigorating and soothing.

Ingredients:

1 teaspoon of yellow tea leaves, 8 ounces of filtered water, 1 tablespoon of orange juice. 1 tablespoon of grapefruit juice, 1 teaspoon of dried chamomile flowers, Orange and grapefruit slices for garnish

Instructions:

Heat the Water: Boil filtered water and let it cool to around 80°C (176°F).

Steep the Tea: Place the yellow tea leaves and dried chamomile flowers in a teapot. Pour the cooled water over the leaves.

Infuse: Allow the tea to steep for 2-3 minutes. Strain the tea into a pitcher.

Mix: Add the orange juice and grapefruit juice to the brewed tea. Stir well to combine.

Serve: Chill the tea in the refrigerator. Serve over ice with slices of orange and grapefruit for a visually appealing and flavorful cooler.

Health Benefits:

This tea cooler provides antioxidants from the yellow tea, vitamin C from the citrus juices, and calming effects from the chamomile flowers.

Interesting Facts:

Combining citrus with yellow tea creates a delightful fusion of flavors, enhancing the tea's natural notes while adding a refreshing twist. Chamomile, traditionally used for relaxation, adds a subtle floral touch to the blend.

As we continue our journey through the world of tea, it's time to venture beyond the familiar realm of tea leaves and explore something equally enchanting—teas without tea leaves. Yes, you read that right! Traditionally, tisanes have been lovingly referred to as tea, even though they don't contain a single tea leaf. Let's step into the vibrant world of tisanes, where the flavors of blossoms, herbs, fruits, and spices come together to create soothing and invigorating brews.

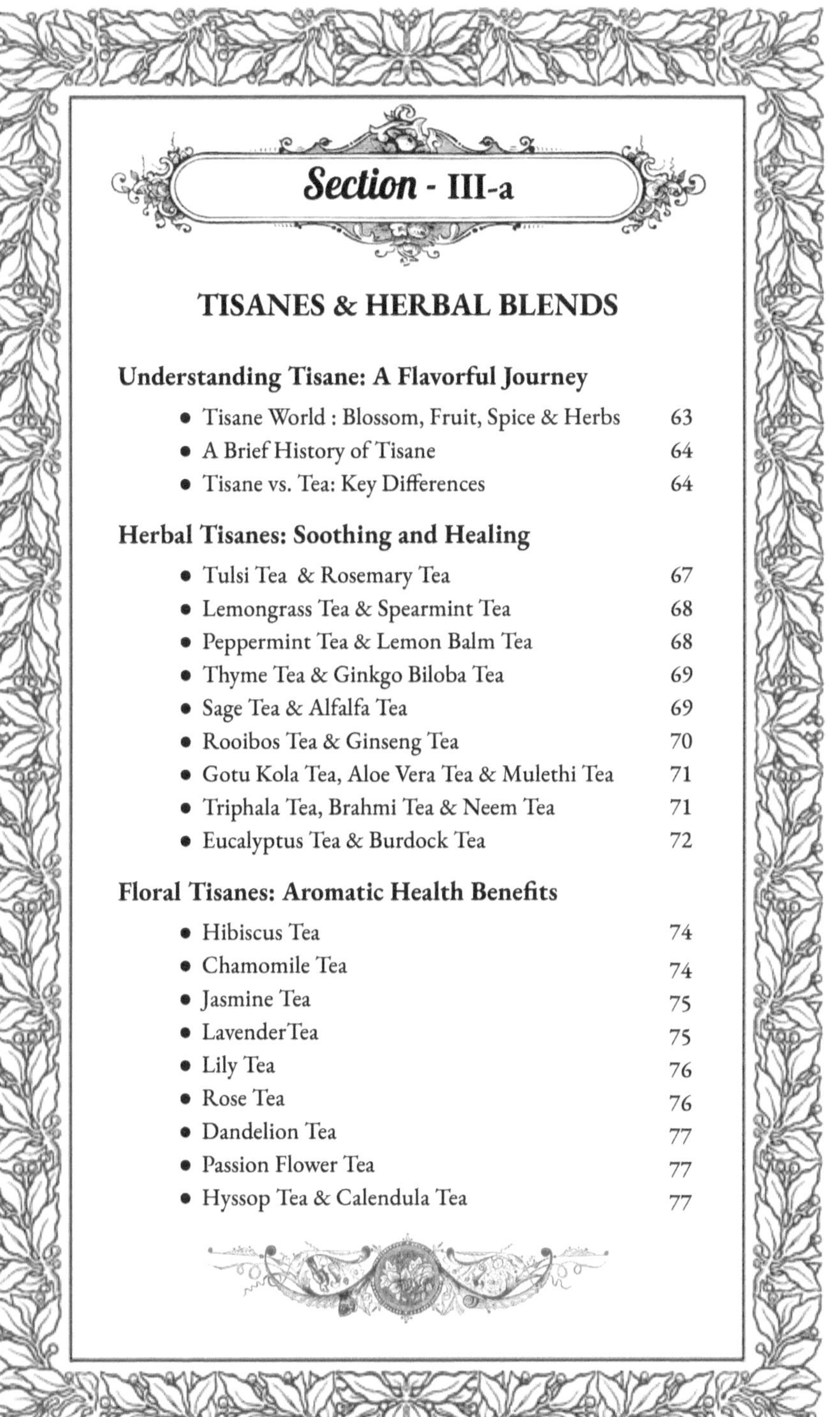

Section - III-a

TISANES & HERBAL BLENDS

"A brief intermission, savor the silence before the next recipe unfolds."

1.5 - UNDERSTANDING TISANE : A FLAVOURFUL JOURNEY

TISANE WORLD : BLOSSOM, FRUITS, SPICES, AND HERBS

isane, pronounced "ti-zahn," is a delightful and versatile beverage made from the infusion of herbs, flowers, fruits, and spices. Unlike traditional teas, which are derived from the leaves of the Camellia sinensis plant, tisanes are caffeine-free and crafted from a diverse array of plant materials.

This characteristic makes tisanes an appealing choice for those seeking flavorful and soothing drinks without the stimulating effects of caffeine. From calming chamomile to invigorating peppermint, tisanes offer an expansive range of flavors and health benefits tailored to suit every palate and need.

As we transition from the rich and varied world of traditional teas, we now embark on an enchanting journey into the diverse realm of tisanes. Having explored the essence of what makes tea a cherished beverage across cultures, we turn our gaze towards its vibrant cousin: the tisane.

While true teas derive from the Camellia sinensis plant, tisanes are crafted from an array of botanicals—herbs, flowers, fruits, and spices. This chapter will delve into the fascinating world of tisanes, revealing their distinct characteristics and the delightful recipes that bring out their unique flavors.

"In the words of herbalist and author Rosemary Gladstar, "Herbs are the friends of the sick, the wise, and the curious. They teach us about ourselves and the world around us." Tisanes, in their many forms, offer a treasure trove of flavors and benefits".

We'll explore the soothing comfort of herbal tisanes, the aromatic charm of floral infusions, the refreshing zest of fruit blends, and the warming embrace of spice concoctions.

Each variety has its own story, often rooted in ancient traditions and cultural practices. For instance, the use of chamomile for relaxation dates back to the ancient Egyptians, while the art of blending spices for health has been celebrated in Ayurvedic medicine for thousands of years.

As we dive into each type, you'll discover not just how to prepare these delightful brews but also the histories and benefits that make them so special. Get ready to be inspired by the herbal magic and botanical wonders that await you in the world of tisanes.

A Brief History of Tisane:

From Ancient Egypt to Modern Times

The history of tisane dates back thousands of years, with roots in ancient civilizations across the globe. In ancient Egypt, herbal infusions were highly valued for both medicinal and ritualistic purposes. As early as 1550 BCE, the Ebers Papyrus, an ancient Egyptian medical text, documented the use of various herbs like peppermint and chamomile for healing and ceremonial uses.

The Greeks and Romans also embraced the therapeutic benefits of herbal teas, incorporating them into their daily lives for health and relaxation. Notably, the Greek physician Hippocrates, often called the "Father of Medicine," recommended the use of herbal infusions for their healing properties around 400 BCE. Similarly, Roman naturalist Pliny the Elder, in his comprehensive work "Naturalis Historia" written in 77 AD, extensively detailed the uses of various herbs in creating beneficial tisanes.

Throughout the Middle Ages, tisanes continued to gain popularity in Europe, particularly within monasteries where monks cultivated extensive herb gardens to create healing infusions. Saint Hildegard of Bingen, a 12th-century German Benedictine abbess, was known for her extensive knowledge of herbal medicine and her writings on the therapeutic uses of plants in tisanes. The Renaissance period saw an expansion in the use of exotic spices and fruits in tisanes, thanks to the flourishing trade routes established by explorers like Marco Polo and Vasco da Gama.

In Asia, tisanes have a rich heritage as well. Traditional Chinese Medicine, with texts dating back to the Han Dynasty (206 BCE – 220 CE), has long utilized herbal infusions for their healing properties. The famous Chinese pharmacopoeia, "Shennong Ben Cao Jing" (The Divine Farmer's Materia Medica), compiled around the 1st century CE, describes numerous herbs used in tisanes for various ailments. Meanwhile, in India, Ayurvedic practices, which have been around for over 5,000 years, incorporate a variety of herbs and spices into soothing brews. The "Charaka Samhita," an ancient Indian Ayurvedic text, details the use of herbs like tulsi (holy basil) and ginger in creating therapeutic infusions.

Tisane vs. Tea: Key Differences

While both tisanes and traditional teas are enjoyed as hot or cold beverages, there are several key differences between the two:

Source Plant:

Traditional teas come exclusively from the Camellia sinensis plant, resulting in green, black, white, and oolong teas depending on the processing method. In contrast, tisanes are made from a wide range of herbs, flowers, fruits, and spices, offering a more diverse selection of ingredients and flavors.

Caffeine Content:

Traditional teas contain varying levels of caffeine, which can provide a stimulating effect. Tisanes, however, are naturally caffeine-free, making them an excellent choice for those looking to avoid caffeine, especially in the evenings or for individuals sensitive to caffeine.

Flavor Profile:

Tisanes offer a broader spectrum of flavors, from fruity and floral to spicy and herbal, depending on the ingredients used. This variety allows for a more customized tea experience, catering to different tastes and preferences.

Health Benefits:

While both traditional teas and tisanes offer health benefits, tisanes are often specifically chosen for their therapeutic properties based on the individual ingredients. For instance, peppermint tisane is known for its digestive benefits, while chamomile is renowned for its calming effects. Traditional teas, on the other hand, generally offer benefits like antioxidants and heart health support.

Cultural Significance:

Traditional teas have a significant cultural heritage, particularly in countries like China, Japan, and India, where tea ceremonies and rituals are an integral part of the culture. Tisanes, while also culturally significant in various regions, are often more associated with medicinal and therapeutic uses across different cultures. Nowadays, tisanes are gaining popularity among the youth and those who appreciate the visual and flavor appeal of tea. While traditional tea is well-established, tisanes offering a diverse and appealing alternative.

Image 2.0 ~Savoring Moments: Two Women Enjoying Tea Together

Herbal Tisanes: Soothing and Healing

Herbs have been cherished for centuries as natural remedies, offering a wide array of flavors and health benefits. These botanical treasures have been used to create tisanes, which are herbal infusions made by steeping various parts of plants, such as leaves, flowers, stems, and roots. Each herb brings its own unique characteristics to the infusion, making herbal tisanes a popular choice for those seeking natural and holistic health solutions.

Herb	Primary Taste	Native Origin	Health Benefit
Tulsi	Spicy and Sweet	India	Supports immunity and stress relief
Rosemary	Piney and Aromatic	Mediterranean	Enhances memory and cognitive function
Lemongrass	Citrusy and Refreshing	Southeast Asia	Aids digestion and reduces inflammation
Spearmint	Mild and Minty	Europe, Asia	Soothes digestion and balances hormones
Peppermint	Cool and Refreshing	Europe, Middle East	Relieves digestive issues and headaches
Lemon Balm	Lemon-like and Mild	Southern Europe	Reduces anxiety and promotes sleep
Lemon Verbena	Lemony and Sweet	South America	Supports digestion and stress relief
Rooibos	Sweet and Earthy	South Africa	Rich in antioxidants, supports heart health
Thyme	Earthy and Minty	Mediterranean	Relieves respiratory issues, antibacterial
Sage	Savory and Earthy	Mediterranean	Anti-inflammatory, supports cognitive health
Ginkgo Biloba	Slightly Bitter	China	Improves circulation and cognitive function
Gotu Kola	Earthy and Bitter	Asia	Enhances memory and reduces anxiety
Alfalfa	Mild and Grassy	Central Asia	Supports overall wellness, rich in vitamins
Aloe Vera	Mild and Slightly Bitter	Arabian Peninsula	Soothes digestion and supports skin health
Ginseng	Bitter and Earthy	Korea, China	Boosts energy and supports immune function
Eucalyptus	Fresh and Minty	Australia	Relieves cold symptoms and respiratory issues
Burdock	Earthy and Slightly Sweet	Europe, Asia	Detoxifies and supports liver health

Table 1.3 ~ Showing herbs, their primary taste, origin and health benefits

Herbal infusions Tisane Recipes:

Following are a few of the most popular herbal infusion tisane recipes, known for their unique flavors and health benefits. These tisanes, made from a variety of herbs, offer a natural and soothing alternative to traditional teas. Whether you seek relaxation, digestive aid, or immune support, these herbal infusions provide a delightful way to enhance your wellness routine.

Tulsi Tea
Bitter | Sharp | Crisp

About :

Tulsi (holy basil), is native to the Indian subcontinent and widespread throughout the Southeast Asian tropics. Tulsi tea is known in the therapy field of Indian ayurvedic as the "queen of herbs". It is a very important plant in the therapy world of Ayurveda, or the "life science". There are 3 types of tulsi available, the green color tulsi known as "Rama Tulsi", the darker and purple color tulsi known as "Krishna Tulsi" and the tulsi grows in forest known as "Vana Tulsi".

Brewing Instructions :

Place 250 ml water in a tea kettle and heat for boiling. Add 10-15 fresh tulsi leaves. Boil for next 10 minutes. Strain and serve with honey and splash of lemon juice as a perfect herbal tea..

Infusion Tip:

You can blend this tea with ginger, green tea or green cardamom for variation in taste and benefits.

Health Benefits :

Helps reduce stress and anxiety,
Calming yet energizing sattvic herb,
Immune modulating adaptogen,
Digestive and respiratory aid

Rosemary Tea
Earthy | Woody | Sharp

About :

Rosemary, is a woody, long lasting herb with fragrant, green, needle-like leaves. The name "rosemary" came from the Latin word "dew of the sea" referring to the fact that this herb grows on cliffs by the sea and is able to survive with humidity from the sea.

Brewing Instructions :

Boil 250 ml water in a tea kettle. Add 10-15 roughly teared fresh or 1 tsp dried rosemary leaves in teapot. Pour the water from kettle. Steep the tea for 5-6 minutes. Strain and serve.

Infusion Tips:

You can blend rosemary tea with chamomile, cardamom, lavender Avoid adding lemon to rosemary tea.

Health Benefits :

Optimizing digestion,
Increasing cognitive function,
Preventing cancer.

Image 2.1
~Rosemary plant
and flower.

Lemongrass Tea
Cituricy | Tangy | Soft

About:
Lemongrass is native to the tropical and subtropical climates of Asia, Australia and Africa. India is the highest producer of lemongrass and use culinary and medicinal herb. Lemongrass is a cooling, clear, and crisp herbal tea with a distinctive, spicy, lemony aroma.

Brewing Instructions:
Boil 250 ml water in a tea kettle. Add 2 tablespoon cup roughly chopped fresh lemongrass leaves in teapot. Pour the water from kettle. Steep the tea for 10 minutes. Strain and serve.

Infusion Tips:
You can blend lemongrass tea with lemon zest, cardamom, ginger, honey and lemon as tastemaker.

Health Benefits:
Weight loss tea,
Improved digestion, Healthy heart.

Spearmint Tea
Pleasant | Sweet | Mild

Brewing Instructions :
Quantity: 1 tsp (fresh) or 1 tsp (dried) Spearmint leaves per 250ml
Water temperature: Boiling (212ºF)
Steeping time: 5 - 10 minutes
Tastemaker: Honey, Lemon
Infusion: lavender, fennel seeds, ginger, citrus fruits
Health Benefits: Relief in nausea, gas, indigestion, headache

Lemon Balm Tea
Citrusy | Fresh | Sweet

Brewing Instructions :
Quantity: 1 tsp (fresh) or 1 tsp (dried) Lemon balm leaves per 250ml
Water temperature: Boiling (212ºF)
Steeping time: 5 - 10 minutes
Tastemaker: Honey, Lemon
Infusion: Rosehips, orange peel, lavender, ginger, citrus fruits
Health Benefits: Cure insomnia, cold, cough, flu, respiratory infection.

Peppermint Tea
Sharp | Intense | Cooling

Brewing Instructions :
Quantity: 1 tsp (fresh) or 1 tsp (dried) Peppermint leaves per 250ml
Water temperature: Boiling (212ºF)
Steeping time: 5 - 10 minutes
Tastemaker: Honey, Lemon
Infusion: Lavender, fennel seeds, ginger, citrus fruits
Health Benefits: Cure bad breath, weight loss, boost immune system

Lemon Verbena Tea
Bright | Lemony | Fresh

Brewing Instructions :
Quantity: 1 tsp (fresh) or 1 tsp (dried) Lemon Verbena leaves per 250ml
Water temperature: Boiling (212ºF)
Steeping time: 5 - 10 minutes
Tastemaker: Honey, Lemon
Infusion: Green tea, rose hips, orange peel, lavender.
Health Benefits:
Reduce inflammation,
boost immunity

Thyme Tea
Subtel | Minty | Earthy

About :

Thyme belongs to mint family and has woody stem and tiny grayish-green leaves. Thyme flowers are lovely white, pink, violet or lilac tones. Thyme has a subtle, dry aroma and a slightly minty flavor. It is most used and loved for cooking and medicinal uses. This tea is also known as "Women's Tea"

Brewing Instructions :

Boil 250 ml water in a tea kettle. Add 2 tsp fresh or 3 tsp dried thyme leaves in teapot. Pour the water from kettle. Steep the tea for 10-15 minutes. Strain and serve.

Infusion Tips:

You can blend sage tea with green tea, cumin, fennel, anise to make variations.

Health Benefits :

Hormonal balance for womens, Respiratory healing, Digestive disorders.

Gingko Biloba Tea
Bitter | Mild | Delicate

Brewing Instructions :

Quantity: 2 tsp (fresh) or 1 tsp (dried) Ginkgo leaves per 250ml

Water temperature: Boiling (212ºF)

Steeping time: 10-12 minutes

Tastemaker: Honey, lemon

Infusion: Peppermint, nettle, ginger, cinnamon

Health Benefits: Cure dementia, alzheimer's, fatigue.

Sage Tea
Strong | Warm | Earthy

About :

Sage is a long lasting, evergreen subshrub, with woody stems, grayish leaves, and blue to purplish flowers. It's a seasoning herb is best known for the peppery flavor it adds to the many dishes where it is used.

Brewing Instructions :

Boil 250 ml water in a tea kettle. Add 2 tsp fresh or 1 tsp dried sage leaves in teapot. Pour the water from kettle. Steep the tea for 10 minutes. Strain and serve.

Infusion Tips:

You can blend sage tea with green tea, chamomile, rosemary or lavender.

Health Benefits :

Digestive problems, Depression, memory loss, Alzheimer's disease.

Image 2.2
~Sage plant and
flower

Alfalfa Tea
Veggie | Mild | Soothing

Brewing Instructions :

Quantity: 1 tsp (dried) Alfalfa leaves per 250ml

Water temperature: Boiling (212ºF)

Steeping time: 10 - 12 minutes

Tastemaker: Honey, Lemon

Infusion: Green tea, peppermint, spearmint

Health Benefits: Increase appetite, recovering weight, natural laxative.

Rooibos Tea
Earthy | Nutty | Tobacco

About :
Rooibos meaning "red bush"; is a broom-like plants growing in South Africa's fynbos. The leaves are used to make a herbal tea that is called as rooibos tea or redbush tea . The tea has been popular in Southern Africa for generations, but is now consumed in many countries worldwide. The tea has a taste and color somewhat similar to hibiscus tea, or an earthy & nutty flavor like yerba mate. It is also one of the best well known herbal teas and possibly the best alternative to black or green tea.

Brewing Instructions :
Place 250 ml water in a tea kettle and heat for boiling. Add 1 tsp of rooibos. Boil for next 10 minutes. Strain and serve with a dash of zest with a slice of lemon. If you want to enjoy the South African way, then add milk and a bit of sugar or honey to make a perfect herbal tea.

Infusion Tip:
You can blend this tea with green tea, sencha tea, peppermint or fruit like elderberry or grapes.

Health Benefits :
Health benefits of red rooibos tea include its ability to cure headaches, insomnia, asthma, eczema, bone weakness, hypertension, allergies, and premature aging. This tea is absolutely free from caffeine content and is also low in tannins. The recommended amount of rooibos herbal tea is 6 cups a day at the most.

Ginseng Tea
Strong | Enticing | Medicinal

About :
Ginseng is a perennial plant with fleshy roots. The roots are light colored and fork-shaped, which may resemble like human body with 2 legs shape. The plant consists of a long stalk with oval-shaped leaves. Ginseng tea is made from a chopped up Ginseng root. Ginseng is available in 3 variety, fresh, white & red ginseng. Maximum ginseng is consumed by China, South Korea, Canada & United State.

Brewing Instructions :
Place 250 ml water in a tea kettle and heat for 190 to 200ºF. Add 1 tsp ginseng root powders in teapot and pour the hot water from kettle. Steep for next 10 minutes. Strain and serve with honey.

Infusion Tip:
You can blend this tea with lemongrass, peppermint, rosehip, ginger, cardamom & can serve with jujube fruits and Korean chestnuts

Health Benefits :
Boosting mental clarity,
Improving diabetes,
Reducing complications from erectile dysfunction,
Prevents fatigue,
Lowers cholesterol,
Reduces inflammation,
Lowers the risk of cancer.

Image 2.3
~ Ginseng Roots & plats.

Gotu Kola Tea
Bitter | Intense | Astringent

Brewing Instructions :
Quantity: 2 tsp (fresh) or 1 tsp (dried) Gotu Kola leaves per 250ml
Water temperature: Boiling (212ºF)
Steeping time: 10-12 minutes
Tastemaker: Honey, Lemon
Infusion: Chamomile, Dandelion, lavender, ginkgo biloba, tulsi
Health Benefits: Anti-inflammatory, cardiovascular health, anti-arthritis

Aloe Vera Tea
Watery | Bitter | Sweet

Brewing Instructions :
Quantity: 1 tsp of aloe vera jelly per 250ml
Water temperature: Boiling (212ºF)
Steeping time: 10 - 12 minutes
Tastemaker: Honey
Infusion: Green tea, black tea, peppermint
Health Benefits: Improving digestion, skin protection, helps menstruation

Mulethi Tea
Herby | Sweet | Tart

Brewing Instructions:
Quantity: 1 tsp mulethi powder/ 250ml
Water temperature: Boiling (212ºF)
Steeping time: 5 - 6 minutes
Tastemaker: Honey
Infusion: Chamomile, ginger, peppermint
Health Benefits:
Cure heartburn, eczema, Low blood pressure

Triphala Tea
Sour | Pungent | Astringent

Brewing Instructions :
Quantity: 1 tsp triphala powder per 250ml
Water temperature: Boiling (212ºF)
Steeping time: 5 - 6 minutes
Tastemaker: Honey
Infusion: Its a combination of amalaki, bibhitaki, haritaki
Health Benefits: Cure inflammation, immune system, detoxification

Brahmi Tea
Bitter | Sweet | Sharp

Brewing Instructions:
Quantity: 2 tsp (fresh) brahmi leaves per 250ml
Water temperature: Boiling (212ºF)
Steeping time: 5 - 6 minutes
Tastemaker: Honey
Infusion: Tulsi, neem ashwagandha, purified butter, black pepper
Health Benefits: Improve Intellect, longevity, rejuvenation

Neem Tea
Bitter | Purifying | Corrective

Brewing Instructions :
Quantity: ¼ tsp neem leaves powder per 250ml
Water temperature: Boiling (212ºF)
Steeping time: 5 - 6 minutes
Tastemake: Honey
Infusion: Black pepper, cinnamon, licorice root, fennel
Health Benefits: Cure infection, malaria, digestive disorders

Eucalyptus Tea
Cooling | Refreshing | Soothing

About :
Eucalyptus is native to Australia. It is famous for its fast growth, The most important part of eucalyptus species is its grey greenish leaves. These are large, thick and leathery, with a distinctive lanceolate shape.

When the leaves are crushed they release a strong fragrance and oil. The leaves are collected and dried to make a healing cup of tea.

Brewing Instructions :
Boil 250 ml water in a tea kettle. Add 1 chopped up eucalyptus leave in teapot. Pour the water from kettle. Steep the tea for 10 minutes. Strain and serve. Add honey as sweetener.

Infusion Tips:
Black tea, chamomile and peppermint

Health Benefits :
Infection fighter,
Digestive aid,
Respiratory Relief: Eucalyptus tea is known for its ability to help clear nasal congestion, soothe sore throats, and alleviate symptoms of respiratory conditions like bronchitis and asthma.

Image 2.4 ~Eucalyptus Leaves

Burdock Tea
Sweet | Mild | Roasted

About :
Burdock belongs to the daisy family, found in abundance in much of the world.

Burdock has round seed pods with spikes and purple grey shade flowers which bloom during summer.

Burdock is a herb with bristly burrs that are known for sticking to your clothes. Its roots, is the most important parts of the plant for medicinal purposes.

Brewing Instructions :
Boil 250 ml water in a tea kettle. 1 tsp dried burdock root powder in teapot. Pour the water from kettle. Steep the tea for 10 minutes. Strain and serve.

Infusion Tips:
Black tea, orange spice tea, chamomile and peppermint, nettle and dandelion root.

Health Benefits :
Anti-inflammatory,
Anti-helminthic,
Anti-cancer.
Detoxification: Burdock tea is known for its detoxifying properties, helping to cleanse the liver and purify the blood by removing toxins from the body

Image 2.5 ~Burdock Flower

Floral Tisanes: Aromatic Health Benefits

Floral tisanes are celebrated for their delicate aromas, vibrant colors, and soothing properties. These infusions, made from the blossoms of various plants, not only create visually stunning teas but also offer a range of health benefits. Flowers like lavender and hibiscus have been used for centuries in traditional medicine and cultural rituals, cherished for their ability to calm the mind, uplift the spirit, and rejuvenate the body.

The natural fragrances of floral tisanes can evoke a sense of tranquility and well-being. For instance, lavender tea is renowned for its calming effects, making it a popular choice for relaxation and sleep enhancement. Hibiscus tea, with its tart and fruity flavor, is not only refreshing but also packed with antioxidants that support cardiovascular health.

Floral infusions can cater to a variety of moods and occasions. Whether you are seeking a moment of peace after a hectic day, a gentle uplift to your spirits, or a refreshing pick-me-up, floral tisanes offer a versatile and delightful way to enhance your daily routine. Let's explore some popular floral tisanes, their primary tastes, native origins, and health benefits.

Some of the most popular Floral Tisanes:

Flower	Primary Taste	Native Origin	Health Benefit
Hibiscus	Tart and Fruity	Africa, Asia	Rich in antioxidants, supports heart health
Chamomile	Mild and Apple-like	Europe, Western Asia	Calming, promotes sleep and reduces anxiety
Jasmine	Sweet and Fragrant	China, Iran	Antioxidant-rich, enhances mood and digestion
Lavender	Floral and Slightly Sweet	Mediterranean	Calming, reduces stress and aids sleep
Lily	Mild and Sweet	Asia	Soothes coughs, promotes relaxation
Rose	Floral and Slightly Sweet	Asia, Europe	Anti-inflammatory, supports skin health
Dandelion	Earthy and Slightly Bitter	Europe, North America	Detoxifying, supports liver health
Passion Flower	Mild and Floral	Southeastern United States	Calming, reduces anxiety and promotes sleep
Hyssop	Minty and Slightly Bitter	Mediterranean	Respiratory support, anti-inflammatory
Calendula	Mild and Peppery	Mediterranean	Anti-inflammatory, supports skin health

Table 1.4 ~ Type of flowers, Primary taste, Origin & Health Benefits

Floral infusions Tisane Recipes:

Following are a few of the most popular floral infusion tisane recipes, each providing a delicate and soothing experience. These tisanes are crafted from fragrant flowers known for their calming properties and subtle flavors. Enjoy the gentle aroma and natural benefits of these herbal infusions, perfect for relaxing moments and enhancing well-being.

Hibiscus Tea
Lemony | Tart | Berry-rich

About:
Hibiscus plant grow in tropical regions and renowned for their large, showy flowers. There are more than 200 type of hibiscus species available but "hibiscus sabdariffa" is the one most commonly used to make tea. Its flower has large, shaped like a trumpet, have 5 or more petals of various colors, like white, pink, red, orange, yellow and purple. It is also known as roselle; flor de Jamaica, karkade, saril and rose mallow.

Brewing Instructions:
Place 250 ml water in a tea kettle and heat for 190 to 200ºF. Add 2 tsp dried hibiscus flower & one small cinnamon stick in teapot and pour the hot water from kettle. Cover the teapot & steep for next 10 minutes. Strain and serve with honey & lemon slice.

Infusion Tip:
You can blend this tea strawberry, cranberry, rose hips, clove, cinnamon and nutmeg.

Aroma Pairing:
You can pair lemon, cilantro, orange peel & cherry with jasmine as per aroma matching.

Chamomile Tea
Earthy | Crisp apple | Airy

About:
Chamomile is a flower with white petals and a yellow center. The name chamomile actually means "ground apple" because this flower fragrance similar to the apple and is grows close to the ground. Chamomile infusion is one of the best herbal teas and also used in aromatherapy. This is also used to make potpourri and highly used in cosmetics for making beauty products and perfumes.

Brewing Instructions:
Place 250 ml water in a tea kettle and heat for 190 to 200ºF. Add 2 tsp dried chamomile flower & one small cinnamon stick & mint leave (optional) in teapot and pour the hot water from kettle. Cover the teapot & steep for next 10 minutes. Strain and serve with honey & lemon slice.

Infusion Tip:
You can blend this tea ginger, peppermint and lemongrass.

Aroma Pairing:
You can pair honey, cupcakes, cream, sugar, egg.

Health Benefits :
High blood pressure,
High cholesterol,
Boosting immune system,
Reduces inflammation,
Speed up the metabolism.

Jasmine Tea
Sweet | Scented | Sensual

About :
Jasmine flower belongs to the olive family, native to tropical and warm temperate regions. Jasmines are widely cultivated for the special fragrance of their flowers & to extract oil & making fragrances.

Brewing Instructions :
Boil 250 ml water in a tea kettle. 2-3 tsp fresh jasmine flowers & ½ tsp green tea in teapot. Pour the water from kettle. Cover & steep the tea for 10 minutes. Strain and serve.

Infusion Tips:
Jasmine tea can be infuse with black tea, green tea or oolong tea.

Food & Aroma Pairing:
Coconut dessert, fresh fruit salad, biscotti & pastries

Health Benefits :
Improve digestion,
Help in weight Loss,
Stress relief. aids in
reducing stress
and anxiety,
while supporting
digestive health.

Image 2.6
~ Jasmine Flower

Health Benefits :
Fights Anxiety,
Improves digestion,
Promotes skin health,
Keeps gum and teeth healthy,
Fight cancer.

Lavender Tea
Aromatic | Light | Soothing

About :
Lavender is a woody flowery shrub native to the Mediterranean region. The purple blue color flowers exude a uniquely floral perfume that is easily identifiable and very much appreciated.

Brewing Instructions :
Boil 250 ml water in a tea kettle. 1-2 tsp dried lavender flowers & ½ tsp green tea in teapot. Pour the water from kettle. Cover & steep the tea for 10 minutes. Strain and serve.

Infusion Tips:
Lavender tea can be infused with chamomile, lemon & honey.

Food & Aroma Pairing:
Chocolate, cookies, salad dressings, ice cream and sorbet.

Health Benefits :
Sedative & pain relief,
Calming tea,
Female tonic.
Anti-inflammatory,
aid in soothing
digestive issues and
headaches.

Image 2.7
~ Lavender Flower

Lily Tea
Delicate | Musky | Sweet

About :
Lily is a flowering plant that grows from bulbs, known for its large and prominent blooms. These flowers are strikingly beautiful and come in an array of colors, including whites, yellows, oranges, pinks, reds, and purples.

Lilies are admired for their vibrant and diverse hues, making them a popular choice in gardens and floral arrangements. The flowers' bold and colorful appearance, coupled with their distinctive shape, adds a touch of elegance and charm to any setting, highlighting the natural beauty of these captivating blooms.

Brewing Instructions :
Boil 250 ml water in a tea kettle. Add 1-2 tsp dried or fresh lily flower in teapot. Pour the water from kettle. Cover & steep the tea for 10 minutes. Strain and serve. Add honey for sweetness (optional).

Infusion Tips:
Lily tea can be infused with green tea, mint, orange, lemon etc.

Food & Aroma Pairing:
Chicken soup, salad, jujubes, squash, dessert.

Health Benefits :
Breaks down kidney stones,
Prevents body water retention,
Treats conjunctivitis.
Rich in antioxidants

Image 2.8
~Lily Flower

Rose Tea
Sweet | Aromatic | Euphoric

About :
Rose tea, also known as rose bud tea, is crafted from whole rose blossoms or dried rose petals. This delicate and aromatic tea, originating from the Middle East, has gained popularity worldwide for its soothing qualities and floral flavor.

Once cherished primarily in Middle Eastern cultures, rose tea is now enjoyed globally, appreciated for its calming effects and subtle, fragrant taste. The gentle infusion of rose petals creates a beverage that is not only visually appealing but also rich in tradition and universally beloved.

Brewing Instructions :
Boil 250 ml water in a tea kettle. Add 1-2 tsp dried rose buds of petals in teapot. Pour the water from kettle. Cover & steep the tea for 10 minutes. Strain and serve.

Infusion Tips:
Rose tea can be infused with chamomile, black tea, telsi, lavender.

Food & Aroma Pairing:
Chocolate, cookies, salad dressings, ice cream and sorbet.

Health Benefits :
Prevents constipation,
Weight loss.
Detox tea. its calming effects can reduce stress and promote relaxation.

Image 2.9 ~
Rose Flower

Dandelion Tea
Peppery | Raw | Bitter

About :
The flower name Dandelion given by a surgeon for its sharp, serrated leaves that recall the teeth of a lion.

In French, lion's tooth is said "dent de lion" or "dande lion", becoming dandelion in modern times. This herb is a perennial, native to Europe and temperate climates with shiny leaves & single flower with lots of thin petals ranging in color from yellow to orange.

Brewing Instructions :
Place 250 ml water in a tea kettle and heat for 190 to 200ºF. Add 1 tsp dried or fresh dandelion flower, leaves & root each and pour the hot water from kettle. Cover the teapot & steep for next 10 minutes. Strain and serve with honey & lemon slice.

Infusion Tip:
You can blend this tea with licorice, green or oolong tea

Food & Aroma Pairing:
You can pair dandelion leaves with potato, cilantro, wine, pasta, garlic, chile, pepper or onion

Health Benefits :
Reduce water retention,
Lower blood pressure,
Regulate blood sugar,
Improve eczema.
Fight inflammation.
rich in antioxidants,
boost immune system

Image 3.0 ~
Dandelion Flower

Passion Flower Tea
Earthy | Pleasant | Mild

Brewing Instructions :
Quantity: 2 tsp (fresh) or 1 tsp (dried) passion flowers per 250ml
Water temperature: boiling (212ºF)
Steeping time: 5 - 10 minutes
Tastemaker: Honey (optional)
Infusion: Chamomile, lemon balm, valerian, mint
Health Benefits: Calming, circulatory tonic, hormone balancing

Calendula Tea
Bitter | Peppery | Tangy

Brewing Instructions :
Quantity: 2 tsp (fresh) or 1 tsp (dried) calendula flowers per 250ml
Water temperature: boiling (212ºF)
Steeping time: 5 - 10 minutes
Tastemaker: Honey, lemon
Infusion: Green tea, rose hips, mint
Health Benefits: Heal ulcers, wounds and hemorrhoids, aid menstruation and discou

Hyssop Tea
Spicy | Bitter | Fresh

Brewing Instructions :
Quantity: 2 tsp (fresh) or 1 tsp (dried) hyssop flowers & leaves per 250ml
Water temperature: boiling (212ºF)
Steeping time: 5 - 10 minutes
Tastemaker: Honey, lemon
Infusion: Horehong, sage, licorice, cinnamon, lemon balm
Health Benefits: Sedative, cardio -vascular health, hormone Balance

As we explored delicious tisanes made from Hibiscus, Chamomile, Jasmine, Lavender, Lily, Rose, Dandelion, Passion Flower, Hyssop, and Calendula. But the world of flower-based teas doesn't stop here—many other edible flowers like elderflower, violet, and honeysuckle can also be used to create refreshing and healthful tisanes.

Each bloom brings its own unique flavor and charm to your cup, so feel free to explore beyond the list we've covered.

To dry your own flowers for tea, simply gather fresh, pesticide-free blooms, and either hang them upside down in a dry place for 1-2 weeks, or use a dehydrator or oven at low temperatures until they're crisp.

However, be mindful to avoid toxic flowers like foxglove, oleander, or lily of the valley, and ensure your flowers are chemical-free. With a little care, you can enjoy an endless variety of floral tisanes at home!

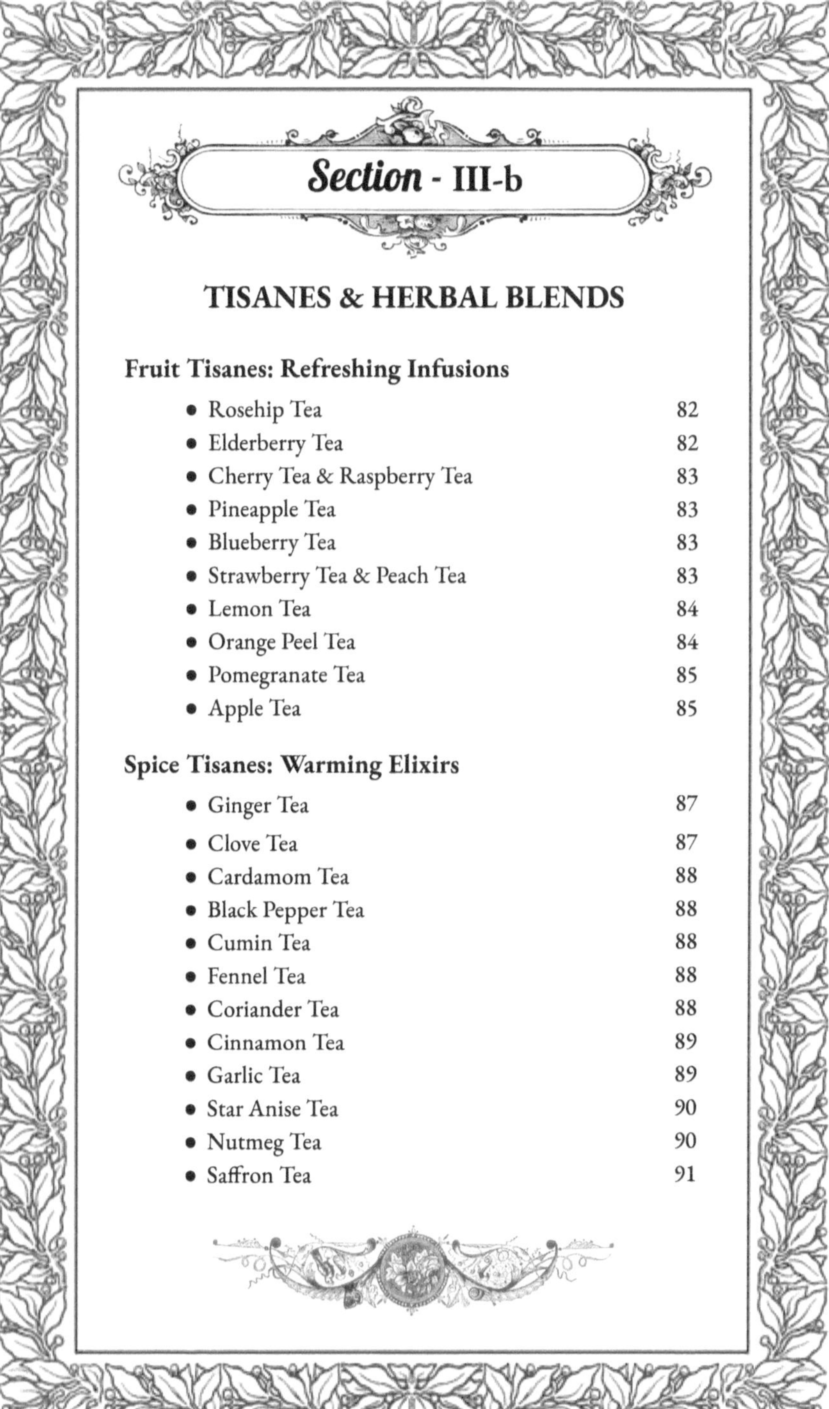

Section - III-b

TISANES & HERBAL BLENDS

Fruit Tisanes: Refreshing Infusions

Spice Tisanes: Warming Elixirs

"Sometimes, even pages need a moment to infuse ideas."

Fruit Tisanes: Refreshing Infusions

Fruit tisanes, also known as fruit teas, are herbal infusions made from a variety of fruits, often combined with other botanicals like flowers and spices. They are naturally caffeine-free and celebrated for their vibrant flavors and refreshing qualities. These tisanes can be served hot to soothe and warm during cooler months, or iced for a cool, refreshing drink in warmer weather.

The appeal of fruit tisanes lies in their versatility and the natural sweetness derived from the fruits. They can be enjoyed on their own or blended with other teas and ingredients to create unique flavor profiles. Additionally, fruit tisanes are often rich in vitamins, antioxidants, and other beneficial compounds, making them a healthful choice.

Some of the most popular Fruit Tisanes:

Fruit Tisane	Primary Taste	Native Origin	Health Benefits
Rosehip Tea	Tangy, Slightly Sweet	Europe, Asia, North Africa	High in vitamin C, antioxidants, anti-inflammatory
Elderberry Tea	Tart, Berry-like	Europe, North America	Immune-boosting, cold and flu relief
Cherry Tea	Sweet, Slightly Tart	Europe, Asia, North America	Rich in antioxidants, high in vitamin C
Blueberry Tea	Sweet, Fruity	North America	High in antioxidants, heart health
Raspberry Tea	Tart, Fruity	Europe, North America	Women's health benefits, rich in vitamins
Strawberry Tea	Sweet, Slightly Tart	Europe, North America	Rich in vitamins and antioxidants
Lemon Tea	Bright, Citrusy	Asia	High in vitamin C, digestive benefits
Orange Peel Tea	Sweet, Tangy	Southeast Asia	High in vitamin C, antioxidants
Pomegranate Tea	Tart, Slightly Sweet	Middle East, South Asia	High in antioxidants, anti-inflammatory
Peach Tea	Sweet, Aromatic	China	Rich in vitamins and antioxidants

Table 1.5 ~ Type of Fruits, Primary taste, Origin & Health Benefits

Fruit infusions Tisane Recipes:

Fruit tisanes are delightful herbal infusions made from a variety of fruits, offering a natural sweetness and vibrant flavors without any caffeine. Versatile and enjoyable both hot and cold, these refreshing beverages are packed with vitamins, antioxidants, and other beneficial compounds. Whether you seek a comforting warm drink or a cool, revitalizing treat, fruit tisanes provide a delicious and healthful option year-round.

Rose Hip Tea
Earthy | Crisp-apple | Airy

About :
Rose is the a very beautiful flower but the fruit rosehip, holds the key to a healthier, fresher more energetic life. Rosehip is the fruit of rose plant, mostly of red color but can be of orange or dark purple color. Wonderfully delicious and filled with the benefits of vitamin C.

Brewing Instructions :
Boil 250 ml water in a tea kettle. Add 4-5 chopped rose hip in teapot. Pour the water from kettle. Cover & steep the tea for 10 minutes. Strain and serve.

Infusion Tips:
You can blend rose hip tea with hibiscus, peppermint, dill, basil & green tea for more variations. You can add lemon and honey as additional tastemaker.

Aroma Pairing:
Rose hip goes well with apple juice, dark rum, croissant, cake, toast, long grain, olive oil, honey, soy drink, apricot, raspberry, cinnamon.

Health Benefits :
Fight off common cold symptoms, Boost immune system.

Elderberry Tea
Tart | Tangy | Bitter

About :
Sambucus is commonly called elder or elderberry is found in the warm regions of Europe and North America. Apart from its medical properties, elderberry fruit is also used for making wine, cordials, marmalade and as a food flavoring.

Brewing Instructions :
Boil 250 ml water in a tea kettle. Add 2 tsp dried berries in teapot. Pour the water from kettle. Cover & Steep the tea for 10 minutes. Strain and serve.

Infusion Tips:
You can blend elderberry tea with green tea, peppermint, lemon balm, vanilla & can add lemon and honey as additional tastemaker.

Aroma Pairing:
Elderberry goes well with darjeeling tea, cava, croissant, honey, mozzarella, soy drink, mango, peppermint, cashew nut, cinnamon.

Health Benefits :
Relief in cold & flu, Reduce inflammation.

Cherry Tea
Tart | Sour | Sweet

Brewing Instructions:
Quantity: 4 tsp crushed cherries per 250ml
Water temperature: boiling (212ºF)
Steeping time: 5 - 10 minutes
Tastemaker: Ginger, honey & lemon
Infusion: Peppermint, clove, lemon balm
Health Benefits: Increase strength, promote brain health

Raspberry Tea
Tart | Fresh | Sweet

Brewing Instructions :
Quantity: 4 tsp crushed berries per 250ml
Water temperature: boiling (212ºF)
Steeping time: 5 - 10 minutes
Tastemaker: Ginger, honey & lemon
Infusion: Lemon balm, mint, cinnamon, cardamom
Health Benefits: Source of nutrients and antioxidants.

Pineapple Tea
Tender | Sweet | Tart

Brewing Instructions :
Quantity: 2 tsp dried pineapple per 250ml
Water temperature: boiling (212ºF)
Steeping time: 5 - 10 minutes
Tastemaker: Honey & lemon
Infusion: Vanilla, ginger, paprika
Health Benefits: Reduces joint pain, keep skin hydrated

Blueberry Tea
Bitter | Sour | Fresh

Brewing Instructions:
Quantity: 4 tsp crushed berries per 250ml
Water temperature: boiling (212ºF)
Steeping time: 5 - 10 minutes
Tastemaker: Ginger, honey & lemon
Infusion: Basil, thyme, cinnamon, cardamom
Health Benefits: Antioxidant, protect cholesterol

Strawberry Tea
Acidic | Sweet | Fruity

Brewing Instructions :
Quantity: 4 tsp crushed berries per 250ml
Water temperature: boiling (212ºF)
Steeping time: 5 - 10 minutes
Tastemaker: Ginger, honey & lemon
Infusion: Black tea, basil, cinnamon, mint.
Health Benefits: No fat, zero cholesterol, free of sodium

Peach Tea
Tart | Mellow | Sweet

Brewing Instructions :
Quantity: 2 tsp dried peach slice per cup (250ml)
Water temperature: boiling (212ºF)
Steeping time: 5 - 10 minutes
Tastemaker: Honey & lemon
Infusion: Black tea, cilantro, cinnamon
Health Benefits: Immune system, dental health, and obesity

Lemon Tea
Tangy | Salty | Bitter

About :
Citrus or lemon is a small yellow juicy fruit native to north eastern India. This fruit is commonly used for culinary, cooking & baking purpose including its juice, zest and pulp.

This is a sour taste fruit and due to its distinctive taste lemon juice become key ingredient in drinks and beverage too. Apart from lemon tea, lemonade (iced) is most popular drink across the world.

Brewing Instructions :
Boil 250 ml water in a tea kettle. Squeeze 1 lemon, add ¼ inch of ginger and 1 tsp honey. Let it boil for another 1 minute. Strain and serve.

Infusion Tips:
Lemon peel tea can be infused with black tea, black pepper, cardamom, cinnamon, tulsi, add honey or sugar as tastemaker.

Aroma Pairing:
Green tea, cake, pasta,
Olive oil, mustard,
Basmati rice, cherry,
Mango, thyme,
Chickpeas, carrot.

Health Benefits :
Cleansing the liver,
Flushing out toxin,
Help in digestion &
weight loss.

Orange Peel Tea
Tangy | Fresh | Bitter

About :
Orange peel is actually the dried skin of an orange or other citrus fruit. The peel itself is quite bitter and not typically eaten raw, but it finds great use in cooking and making tea.

The dried peel adds a unique, tangy flavor to dishes and beverages, infusing them with the essence of citrus.

While it may not be appetizing to eat on its own, when incorporated into recipes, it enhances the flavor profile with its aromatic and slightly bitter notes.

Brewing Instructions :
Boil 250 ml water in a tea kettle. Add 2 tsp dried orange peel. Pour the water from kettle. Cover & Steep the tea for 10 minutes. Strain and serve.

Infusion Tips:
Orange peel tea can be infused with black tea, star anise, cinnamon, cardamom, add honey or sugar as tastemaker.

Aroma Pairing:
Green tea, cake, pastries,
Sweets, basmati rice,
Cherry, peanut, carrot.

Health Benefits :
Improve lung health,
Aids diabetes Treatment,
Help in weight loss.

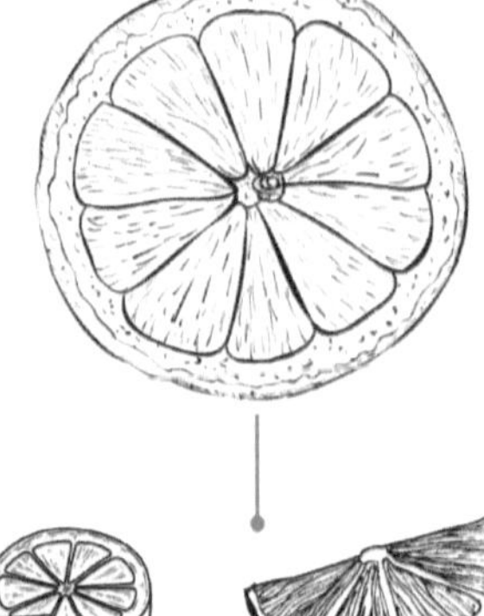

Image 3.1 ~Lemon and Orange Fruit

Pomegranate Tea
Musty | Fruity | Sweet

About :
Pomegranate tea, made from Punica granatum, is derived from the vibrant fruit that, when split open, reveals clusters of juicy, gem-like seeds inside. This fruit is not only enjoyed for its refreshing taste but is also deeply rooted in the Ayurveda system of traditional medicine.

In Ayurveda, pomegranate is valued for its numerous health benefits and is often used to support digestion, heart health, and overall wellness. The tea made from pomegranate seeds or peel carries these beneficial properties, making it a popular choice for those seeking both flavor and health benefits.

Brewing Instructions :
Boil 250 ml water in a tea kettle. Add 4-5 tsp crushed pomegranate seeds. Pour the water from kettle. Cover & Steep the tea for 10 minutes. Strain and serve.

Infusion Tips:
This tea be infused with star anise, coriander, cardamom, add honey or sugar as tastemaker.

Aroma Pairing:
Green tea, coffee, tortilla, brown rice, honey, peppermint, walnut & tomato.

Health Benefits :
Cancer prevention, Anti-inflammatory, Antioxidants.

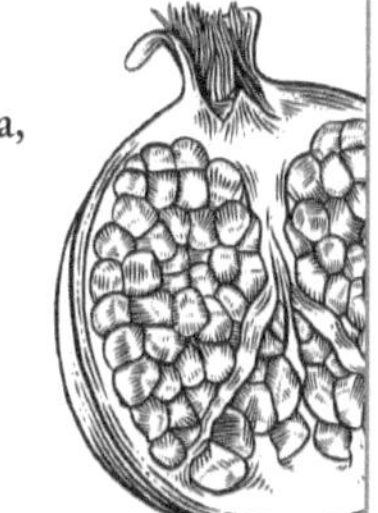

Image 3.2
~ Pomegranate Fruit

Apple Tea
Juicy | Crispy | Crunchy

About :
Apple tea is a soothing beverage made from dried apple pieces, often infused with spices like cinnamon, offering a warm, comforting flavor. It's known for its antioxidant properties and can support digestion and overall wellness.

Brewing Instructions:
Quantity: 2 tsp dried apple per cup (250ml)
Water temperature: boiling (212ºF)
Steeping time: 5 - 10 minutes
Tastemaker: Honey & lemon
Infusion: Black tea, mint, clove, cinnamon
Health Benefits: Weight loss, immunity, vitamin C

Pear Tea
Juicy | Sweet | Mild

About:
Pear tea offers a delicate, sweet flavor and is rich in vitamins, making it a refreshing and nourishing drink.

Brewing Instructions:
Quantity: 2 tsp dried pear per 250ml
Water temperature: boiling (212ºF)
Steeping time: 5 - 10 minutes
Tastemaker: Honey & lemon
Infusion: Black tea, parsley, mint

Health Benefits:
Aid for cataracts & alzheimer.

Image 3.3
~Pear Fruit

Spice Tisanes: Warming Elixirs

Spice tisanes are aromatic and invigorating herbal infusions crafted from a variety of spices, each bringing its unique flavor and therapeutic properties to the brew. These tisanes can be enjoyed both hot and cold, offering a comforting warmth in cooler months and a refreshing kick when served chilled.

The robust and complex flavors of spices like ginger, cinnamon, and turmeric not only create delightful drinks but also provide numerous health benefits, making spice tisanes a popular choice among tea enthusiasts.

Spices have been valued for centuries not only for their culinary uses but also for their medicinal properties. Rich in antioxidants, anti-inflammatory compounds, and essential vitamins and minerals, spice tisanes can help boost the immune system, improve digestion, and enhance overall well-being. Whether you are looking for a soothing beverage to unwind or a revitalizing drink to start your day, spice tisanes offer a flavorful and healthful option.

Some of the most popular Spice Tisanes:

Spice Tisane	Primary Taste	Native Origin	Health Benefits
Ginger Tea	Spicy, Warming	Southeast Asia	Anti-inflammatory, aids digestion, relieves nausea
Clove Tea	Warm, Spicy	Indonesia	Antioxidant-rich, improves digestion, anti-inflammatory
Cardamom Tea	Sweet, Spicy	India	Digestive aid, anti-inflammatory, boosts metabolism
Black Pepper Tea	Spicy, Pungent	India	Improves digestion, antioxidant, anti-inflammatory
Fennel Tea	Sweet, Licorice-like	Mediterranean	Aids digestion, relieves bloating, antioxidant
Cumin Tea	Earthy, Warm	Middle East	Aids digestion, boosts metabolism, rich in iron
Coriander Tea	Citrusy, Earthy	Southern Europe, North Africa	Aids digestion, anti-inflammatory, antioxidant
Cinnamon Tea	Sweet, Spicy	Sri Lanka, India	Antioxidant, anti-inflammatory, regulates blood sugar
Garlic Tea	Pungent, Savory	Central Asia	Boosts immune system, antioxidant, anti-inflammatory
Turmeric Tea	Earthy, Bitter	South Asia	Anti-inflammatory, antioxidant, improves brain function

Table 1.6~ Type of Spices, Primary taste, Origin & Health Benefits

Spice infusions Tisane Recipes:

Following are the most popular spice tisane recipes, each offering a unique blend of aromatic flavors and therapeutic benefits. These tisanes are crafted from a variety of spices known for their robust tastes and health-enhancing properties. Enjoy the warmth and richness of these herbal infusions, whether you seek a soothing drink to relax or a revitalizing brew to invigorate your senses.

Ginger Tea
Hot | Spicy | Juicy

About :
Ginger is considered one of the strongest and most pungent among of all herb also known as hot root. Ginger has been used for many centuries by a great number of peoples around the world for medical & culinary treatments.

Brewing Instructions :
Boil 250 ml water in a tea kettle. Add 1 inch ginger root crushed in teapot. Pour the water from kettle. Cover & steep the tea for 10 minutes. Strain and serve.

Infusion Tips:
You can blend ginger with cinnamon, cardamom & black tea for more variations. Lemon and honey as optional.

Aroma Pairing:
Cardamom, peanut, cake, tortilla, basmati rice, mustard, milk chocolate, butter, oyster, tangy fruits, carrot, mushroom.

Health Benefits :
Improve digestion, weight loss tea,
Nausea relief, boost your immune system,
Colds, flu, fevers and other respiratory issues,
Circulation and heart.

Clove Tea
Pungent | Strong | Astringent

About :
Syzygium aromaticum, commonly known as clove, is widely cherished as an aromatic spice. Clove is actually the dried flower bud of the clove tree, and its strong, pungent flavor makes it a key ingredient in many culinary traditions. Clove oil, is renowned for its medicinal properties, often used to alleviate toothaches and digestive issues.

Brewing Instructions :
Boil 250 ml water in a tea kettle. Add 1 tsp powdered clove (5-6 cloves) in teapot. Pour the water from kettle. Cover & steep the tea for 10 minutes. Strain and serve.

Infusion Tips:
Black tea, cardamom, cinnamon, lemon, honey or sugar as tastemaker.

Aroma Pairing:
Green Tea, apple juice, tequila, gingerbread, cake, rice, pasta, mustard, dark chocolate, cheese.

Health Benefits :
Anti-inflammatory,
Help to resist toxicity,
Pain reliever.

Cardamom Tea
Citrucity | Minty | Spicy

About :
Elettaria cardamomum or cardamom is among the costliest spices found on earth. It's used as cooking and flavourings spices in both food and drink.

Brewing Instructions :
Boil 250 ml water in a tea kettle. Add powdered seeds of 1 cardamom in teapot. Pour the water from kettle. Cover & steep the tea for 10 minutes. Strain and serve.

Infusion Tips:
Black tea, ginger, cinnamon, clove, lemon, honey or sugar as tastemaker.

Aroma Pairing:
Green tea, toast, basmati rice, olive, milk chocolate, mozzarella, grapefruit, chickpeas.

Health Benefits :
Detox tea, cure for bad breath

Black Pepper Tea
Woody | Piney | Sharp

Brewing Instructions :
Quantity: 5-6 crushed black pepper per 250ml
Water temperature: boiling (212ºF)
Steeping time: 5 - 10 minutes
Tastemaker: Ginger, honey & lemon
Infusion: Cinnamon, nutmeg, cumin
Health Benefits: Easing sinus pressure, reducing joint stiffness

Cumin Tea
Earthy | Nutty | Spicy

Brewing Instructions :
Quantity: 2 tsp (fresh) or 1 tsp dried passion flowers per 250ml
Water temperature: boiling (212ºF)
Steeping time: 5 - 10 minutes
Tastemaker: Honey & lemon
Infusion: Cinnamon, clove, nutmeg, cardamom
Health Benefits: Promote digestion, source of iron, weight loss

Fennel Tea
Sweet | Perfumy | Anise-like

Brewing Instructions :
Quantity: 1 tsp crushed fennel seed per 250ml
Water temperature: boiling (212ºF)
Steeping time: 5 - 10 minutes
Tastemaker: Honey & lemon
Infusion: Star anise, clove, fennel
Health Benefits: Heart health, increase fiber, prevent anemia

Coriander Tea
Citrucy | Curry | Sweet

Brewing Instructions :
Quantity: 2 tsp dried crushed coriander seeds per 250ml
Water temperature: boiling (212ºF)
Steeping time: 5 - 10 minutes
Tastemaker: Honey & lemon
Infusion: Turmeric, cumin, cardamom, fennel
Health Benefits:
Treat anemia, stomach disorder, heals ulcers

Cinnamon Tea
Sweet | Savory | Aromatic

About :

Cinnamomum verum or cinnamon is actually an inner bark of the specific tree. This is highly popular aromatic spice used in sweet & savory recipes & to make warming, scented sweet teas & chai tea. It was first cultivated in Sri Lanka and then introduced to India. Cinnamon also represent a tone of mid brown color.

Brewing Instructions :

Boil 250 ml water in a tea kettle. Add 1 small stick or 1 tsp powder in teapot. Pour the water from kettle. Cover & steep the tea for 10 minutes. Strain and serve.

Infusion Tips:

You can blend cinnamon tea with ginger, cardamom, chamomile, peppermint & black tea for more variations. You can add lemon and honey as additional tastemaker.

Aroma Pairing:

Green tea, raspberry, mint, croissant, quinoa, mustard, soya sauce, caramel, honey, butter, star anise, cumin.

Health Benefits :

Improve digestion, weight loss tea,
Aid blood sugar levels
Cure diabetes,
Colds, flu, fevers and other respiratory Issues,
Good for circulation and heart,
Calming effect.

Image 3.3
~Cinnamon Spice

Garlic Tea
Heated | Strong | Spicy

About :

Allium sativum, commonly known as garlic, is a pungent and flavorful herb native to Central Asia.
It is a member of the Allium family, which includes other well-known cooking herbs such as onions, chives, shallots, and leeks. Garlic has been used for centuries in various cuisines around the world, adding a distinctive, aromatic flavor to dishes.
Closely related to its Allium cousins, garlic not only enhances the taste of food but also offers numerous health benefits.

Brewing Instructions :

Boil 250 ml water in a tea kettle. Add 1 crushed garlic clove in teapot. Pour the water from kettle. Cover & steep the tea for 10 minutes. Strain and serve.

Infusion Tips:

Garlic tea can be infused with ginger, lemon & honey or sugar as tastemaker.

Aroma Pairing:

Onions, tomatoes, chilli, ginger, basil, turmeric, beans, chicken, pork and seafood

Health Benefits :

Heart & blood health,
Digestion problem,
Infection fighter.
Good for circulation and heart,
Calming effect.

Image 3.4
~ Garlic Spice

Star Anise Tea
Luxurious | Herbal | Sweet

About :

Illicium verum, commonly known as star anise, is a striking star-shaped fruit with seeds that has captivated cultures around the world for centuries.

This spice is renowned not only for its distinctive shape but also for its warm, licorice-like flavor, making it a popular ingredient in both traditional medicine and global cuisine.

Star anise is often used to add depth and complexity to a variety of dishes, from savory stews to sweet desserts.

Brewing Instructions :

Boil 250 ml water in a tea kettle. Add 1 or 2 start pods in teapot. Pour the water from kettle. Cover & steep the tea for 10 minutes. Strain and serve.

Infusion Tips:

Star anise tea can be infused with green tea, rosemary, thyme, sage, lemon & honey or sugar as tastemaker.

Aroma Pairing:

Green tea, corn tortilla, pasta, mustard, milk chocolate, mango, blackcurrant, walnut

Health Benefits :
Disestion,
Respiratory ailments,
Hormone simulation.
Relieves bloating, gas,
and indigestion.
Used in traditional
medicine for coughs
and bronchitis.

Image 3.5 ~ Star Anise Spice

Nutmeg Tea
Mysterious | Unique | Sweet

About :

fruit is known as mace, while the internal part is referred to as nutmeg. This versatile spice is not only valued for its culinary uses but is also commercially utilized to produce essential oils and nutmeg butter.

Nutmeg and mace are both treasured for their warm, aromatic flavor, which enhances a wide variety of dishes and beverages. Nutmeg is a very popular spice used in Indian cuisines especially sweet preparations.

Brewing Instructions :

Boil 250 ml water in a tea kettle. Add ¼ tsp nutmeg powder. Pour the water from kettle. Cover & steep the tea for 10 minutes. Strain and serve.

Infusion Tips:

Nutmeg tea can be infused with black tea, star anise, cinnamon, cumin, add honey or sugar as tastemaker.

Aroma Pairing:

Green tea, almond cookies, pasta, mustard, milk chocolate, orange peel, lime, rosemary.

Health Benefits :
Calming,
Circulatory tonic.
Contains antioxidants
that strengthen the
immune system.
Supports liver health and helps flush out toxins. Contains compounds that have a calming effect, aiding in better sleep.

Image 3.6 ~Nutmeg Spice

Saffron Tea
Floral | Musky | Aromatic

About :
The Crocus sativus flower is renowned for its vivid crimson stigmas and styles, known as threads, which, when carefully plucked and dried, transform into saffron—one of the most expensive and sought-after species globally. Saffron is cherished not only for its rich, golden color but also for its unique and delicate flavor, making it an essential ingredient in a wide range of culinary dishes across various cultures. It is commonly used as both a seasoning and a natural coloring agent in cuisines from the Mediterranean to the Middle East and beyond.

Iran stands as the leading producer of saffron, supplying the majority of the world's demand with exceptional quality and volume. Meanwhile, Spain plays a significant role as the largest importer of this valuable spice, using it extensively in traditional dishes like paella. India, particularly the Kashmir region, is also renowned for producing high-quality saffron, often referred to as "Kashmiri saffron," which is highly prized for its deep color and strong aroma, making it a staple in Indian cuisine and traditional medicine.

Brewing Instructions :

Boil Water: Bring 250 ml of water to a boil in a tea kettle.
Prepare Saffron: Place 0.25 grams of saffron threads in a teapot.
Pour Water: Carefully pour the boiling water over the saffron threads in the teapot.
Steep: Cover the teapot and allow the saffron to steep for 10 minutes.
Strain & Serve: Strain the tea into cups and serve immediately. Enjoy your saffron tea!

Infusion Tips:
You can blend saffron tea with cinnamon, ginger, anise, fennel, cardamom, peppermint & green tea for more variations. You can add lemon and honey as additional tastemaker.

Aroma Pairing:
Saffron goes well with asparagus, rice, eggs, cheese, chicken, leeks, seafood, mushrooms and spinach and pairs nutmeg, paprika and pepper too.

Health Benefits :
Protects against cancer,
Promotes learning and memory retention,
Increase vitality,
Protection against cold,
Antidepressants.

Image 3.7 ~Saffron Flower

Unique Indigenous Blends

Fruit tisanes, also known as fruit teas, are herbal infusions made from a variety of fruits, often combined with other botanicals like flowers and spices. They are naturally caffeine-free and celebrated for their vibrant flavors and refreshing qualities. These tisanes can be served hot to soothe and warm during cooler months, or iced for a cool, refreshing drink in warmer weather.

The appeal of fruit tisanes lies in their versatility and the natural sweetness derived from the fruits. They can be enjoyed on their own or blended with other teas and ingredients to create unique flavor profiles. Additionally, fruit tisanes are often rich in vitamins, antioxidants, and other beneficial compounds, making them a healthful choice.

Golden Turmeric Elixir Recipe

Golden Turmeric Elixir is a warm, soothing drink that harnesses the powerful anti-inflammatory and antioxidant properties of turmeric. This golden-hued beverage is often enjoyed for its health benefits and comforting flavor.

Ingredients:

1 cup of coconut milk (or any plant-based milk)

1 teaspoon of ground turmeric

1/2 teaspoon of ground ginger

1/4 teaspoon of ground cinnamon

1 tablespoon of honey or maple syrup

Image 38 ~ Ginger Spice

A pinch of black pepper (enhances the absorption of curcumin from turmeric)

Optional: a small piece of fresh turmeric and ginger, grated

Instructions:

Heat the Milk: In a small saucepan, gently heat the coconut milk over medium heat until warm.

Add the Spices: Add the ground turmeric, ground ginger, ground cinnamon, and black pepper. Whisk continuously until the spices are well incorporated and the milk is hot but not boiling.

Sweeten: Stir in the honey or maple syrup to taste. If using fresh turmeric and ginger, add them at this stage and let simmer for a few minutes.

Serve: Pour the golden elixir into a mug and enjoy warm.

Health Benefits: Turmeric is renowned for its curcumin content, which has potent anti-inflammatory and antioxidant effects. This elixir can help reduce inflammation, boost immune function, and improve digestion. Ginger adds additional anti-inflammatory benefits and aids in digestion, while cinnamon helps regulate blood sugar levels.

Fact: In traditional Ayurvedic medicine, turmeric has been used for thousands of years for its healing properties. The addition of black pepper enhances curcumin absorption by up to 2,000%, making this drink both a health powerhouse and a flavorful treat.

Floral Hibiscus Punch Recipe

Floral Hibiscus Punch is a vibrant and refreshing drink that combines the tartness of hibiscus flowers with the subtle sweetness of other botanicals. This ruby-red beverage is perfect for hot days and is a delightful way to enjoy the benefits of hibiscus.

Ingredients:

1/4 cup of dried hibiscus flowers

4 cups of water

1/2 cup of fresh mint leaves

1/4 cup of honey or agave syrup

1/2 cup of fresh orange juice

1/4 cup of fresh lime juice

Ice cubes

Orange and lime slices for garnish & fresh mint sprigs for garnish

Image 3.9 ~Hibiscus Flower

Instructions:

Brew the Hibiscus Tea: Bring the water to a boil, then remove from heat and add the dried hibiscus flowers and fresh mint leaves. Let steep for 10-15 minutes.

Strain and Sweeten: Strain the tea into a pitcher and discard the hibiscus flowers and mint leaves. Stir in the honey or agave syrup until dissolved.

Add Citrus Juices: Add the fresh orange juice and lime juice to the hibiscus tea. Stir well to combine.

Chill: Refrigerate the punch until it is well chilled.

Serve: Serve over ice cubes and garnish with orange and lime slices and fresh mint sprigs.

Health Benefits: Hibiscus tea is rich in antioxidants and vitamin C, which support immune health and skin health. It also has been shown to help lower blood pressure and cholesterol levels. The addition of mint provides a refreshing taste and can aid in digestion.

Fact: Hibiscus tea is popular worldwide, known as "sorrel" in the Caribbean, "karkade" in Egypt, and "agua de Jamaica" in Mexico. It has been enjoyed for centuries for its vibrant color, tart flavor, and health benefits.

Ginger and Lemongrass Zest Recipe

Ginger and Lemongrass Zest is a revitalizing tisane that combines the spicy warmth of ginger with the citrusy freshness of lemongrass. This invigorating beverage is perfect for a morning pick-me-up or an afternoon refresher.

Ingredients:

1 tablespoon of fresh ginger, thinly sliced

2 stalks of fresh lemongrass, chopped

4 cups of water

1-2 tablespoons of honey or maple syrup & fresh lemon slices for garnish

Instructions:

Prepare the Ingredients: Thinly slice the ginger and chop the lemongrass stalks.

Boil the Water: Bring the water to a boil in a medium-sized pot.

Steep the Tisane: Add the ginger and lemongrass to the boiling water. Reduce heat and let simmer for 10-15 minutes.

Strain and Sweeten: Strain the tisane into a teapot or pitcher, discarding the ginger and lemongrass pieces. Stir in the honey or maple syrup to taste.

Serve: Pour into cups and garnish with fresh lemon slices if desired. Enjoy warm or chilled over ice.

Health Benefits: Ginger is well-known for its anti-inflammatory and digestive benefits, while lemongrass aids in detoxification and has antimicrobial properties. This combination makes for a soothing and health-boosting beverage that can help alleviate nausea, reduce inflammation, and support overall wellness.

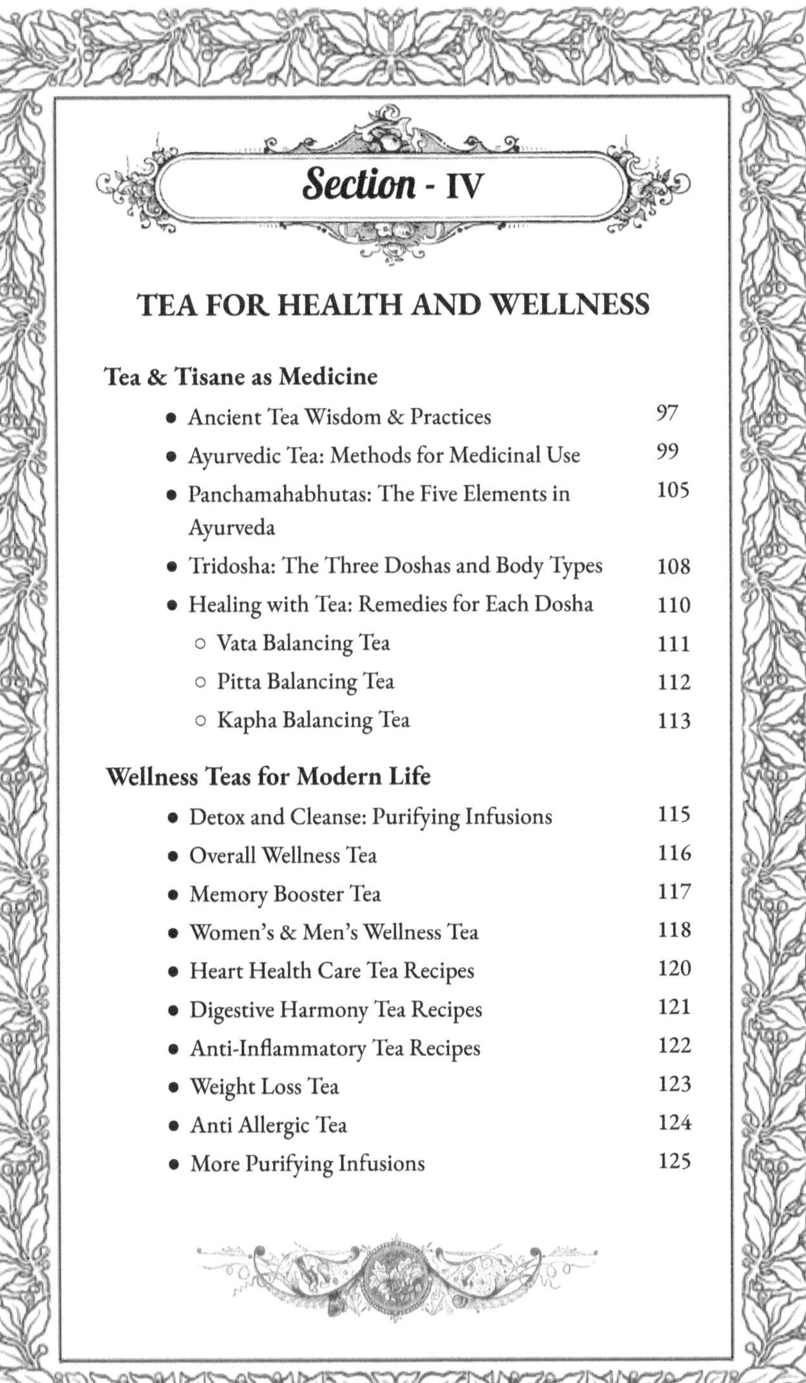

Section - IV

TEA FOR HEALTH AND WELLNESS

"Patience is key, even in tea and empty pages."

1.6 - TEA & TISANE AS MEDICINE

ANCIENT TEA WISDOM & PRACTICES

ea and tisane has long been cherished not only for its soothing flavors but also for its medicinal properties. For thousands of years, civilizations around the world have utilized tea and tisane as a natural remedy to promote health and well-being.

The earliest records of tea as medicine date back to ancient China, where it was initially consumed as a tonic. Legends tell of Emperor Shen Nong, who discovered the healing power of tea around 2737 BCE. He found that boiling water with leaves from a wild tea tree produced a drink that invigorated the body and soothed the mind. This early use of tea laid the foundation for a rich tradition of herbal medicine that spread across Asia and beyond.

The Ancient Practices of China and India

In China, the practice of using herbs and tisanes (herbal teas) for healing has evolved over millennia. Traditional Chinese Medicine (TCM) incorporates a variety of herbal teas to balance the body's qi (vital energy) and treat ailments ranging from digestive issues to respiratory problems. These herbal concoctions are often tailored to the individual's specific health needs, emphasizing a holistic approach to wellness.

India, too, boasts a profound history of utilizing herbs in its ancient healing system known as Ayurveda. This centuries-old practice emphasizes the balance of mind, body, and spirit, using a variety of natural remedies including herbal teas. Ayurvedic teas, made from a blend of spices, herbs, and plants, are designed to balance the body's doshas (biological energies) and promote overall health. For instance, ginger tea is commonly used to aid digestion, while tulsi (holy basil) tea is renowned for its stress-relieving properties.

The Wisdom of Ayurveda

Ayurveda, which means "Science of life," is a holistic healing system that has been practiced in India for over 5,000 years. It views health as a harmonious balance between the five elements (earth, water, fire, air, and ether) and the three doshas (Vata, Pitta, and Kapha). Ayurvedic teas are crafted to balance these elements and doshas, supporting the body's natural healing processes. These teas not only address physical ailments but also nurture mental and emotional well-being, reflecting Ayurveda's comprehensive approach to health.

Greek and Roman Contributions

The ancient Greeks and Romans also recognized the medicinal properties of tea. Hippocrates, often called the "Father of Medicine," documented the use of herbal infusions to treat various ailments. The Romans, influenced by Greek medical practices, adopted the use of herbal teas in their own healthcare routines. They believed in the restorative powers of herbs such as chamomile, mint, and fennel, which were used to ease digestion, calm the mind, and promote restful sleep.

A Word of Caution

As we embark on this exploration of tea as medicine, it is important to note that the information presented in this book is based on traditional knowledge passed down through generations. These recipes and practices are part of a cultural heritage, shared from grandmother to mother to author. While these herbal teas have been cherished for their natural benefits and are generally considered safe, they are not a substitute for professional medical advice.

> *"In the chapters that follow, you will discover a variety of tea recipes designed to address common health concerns and enhance daily life. However, please remember that this text is not intended as a doctor's prescription. The author is not a trained medical expert, and the information provided should not be used as a substitute for consulting a qualified healthcare professional. If you have any health concerns or medical conditions, it is always best to seek the advice of a knowledgeable vaidya (Ayurvedic practitioner) or a doctor".*

Looking Ahead

In the upcoming chapters, we will explore the fascinating world of Ayurveda in greater detail. You will learn about the five elements that form the foundation of Ayurvedic philosophy, the three doshas that govern our physical and mental health, and how to use herbal teas to restore balance and vitality.

From calming teas for stress relief to invigorating blends for boosting energy, you will find recipes to support your well-being in every aspect of life. Join us on this journey to discover the ancient wisdom of tea as medicine and unlock the natural healing power that lies within each cup.

Ayurvedic Tea: Methods for Medicinal Use

Ayurvedic tea or **"Healing teas"** are a natural way to support health and well-being, utilizing the medicinal properties of various herbs and spices. These teas can be prepared using several methods to maximize the extraction of beneficial compounds.

The most common techniques include infusions, decoctions, fomentations, and the preparation of herbal juices, oils, and ointments. Each method is tailored to the specific properties of the herbs being used, ensuring that the active ingredients are effectively harnessed.

Below, we explore these methods in detail, providing step-by-step processes, appropriate measurements, temperature guidelines, and examples of herbs and their uses.

Infusions

Infusions are one of the simplest and most effective methods for extracting the beneficial properties of herbs, especially for delicate plant parts like leaves and flowers. This method involves steeping the herbs in water to draw out their medicinal compounds. Infusions can be prepared as hot, cold, or a combination of both hot and cold infusions.

Hot Infusion

One of excellent herb for hot infusion is Chamomile. Chamomile tea is renowned for its calming and soothing properties, perfect choice for relaxation and sleep support.

Preparation Steps:

Boil Water: Bring water to a boil, then let it cool slightly to just below boiling point (around 200°F or 93°C).

Measure Herbs: Use about one teaspoon of dried chamomile flowers (or one tablespoon of fresh flowers) per cup of water.

Combine and Steep: Place the chamomile flowers in a teapot or mug. Pour the hot water over the flowers, ensuring they are fully submerged. Cover the teapot or mug to retain the heat and volatile oils.

Steep Time: Let the chamomile steep for 5-10 minutes. This duration is typically sufficient to extract the soothing properties without making the tea too bitter.

Strain and Serve: After steeping, strain the flowers using a fine mesh strainer or cheesecloth, and enjoy your chamomile tea.

Use Case Example

Chamomile Tea: Known for its gentle, calming effects, chamomile tea can help ease anxiety, improve sleep quality, and soothe digestive issues.

Cold Infusion

Peppermint is a versatile herb known for its refreshing flavor and soothing properties. When prepared as a cold infusion, it provides a cooling and invigorating beverage, ideal for hot weather or as a revitalizing drink throughout the day.

Preparation Steps:

Measure Herbs: Place about one teaspoon of dried peppermint leaves (or one tablespoon of fresh peppermint leaves) into a jar or pitcher.

Add Water: Fill the jar or pitcher with cold, filtered water.

Steep: Cover the jar or pitcher and refrigerate it. Allow the peppermint to infuse in the cold water for several hours or overnight.

Strain and Serve: After the infusion period, strain the peppermint leaves using a fine mesh strainer or cheesecloth. Serve the chilled tea over ice if desired.

Use Case Example:

Peppermint cold infusion is not only a delightful and refreshing summer drink but also offers several health benefits. The menthol in peppermint provides a cooling effect that can help relieve nausea and ease digestive discomfort. Additionally, it aids in reducing headaches and provides a natural boost of energy.

Hot and Cold Infusion

Another excellent herb for a hot and cold infusion is Hibiscus. Hibiscus tea is known for its tart, cranberry-like flavor and vibrant red color. It is rich in antioxidants and can be enjoyed both hot and cold, making it a versatile choice. This herbal tea can be made by using hot and cold infusion.

Preparation Steps:

Start with Hot Water: Steep the hibiscus flowers in hot water for 5-10 minutes, using about one teaspoon of dried hibiscus flowers (or one tablespoon of fresh flowers) per cup of water.

Cool Down: After the initial hot steeping, transfer the hot infusion to a container filled with cold water or ice to rapidly cool it down.

Complete Steeping: Allow the infusion to cool completely, either at room temperature or in the refrigerator.

Strain and Serve: Once the infusion has cooled, strain the flowers and enjoy your hibiscus tea.

Use Case Example

Hibiscus Tea: This vibrant tea can be enjoyed hot for a warming, tart drink, or cold for a refreshing, hydrating beverage. Hibiscus tea is very tasty, smooth in flavour, packed with antioxidants and is known for its ability to help lower blood pressure, making it a great choice for heart health.

Decoctions and Fomentations

Decoctions and fomentations are methods used to extract the medicinal properties of tougher plant materials such as roots, bark, and seeds. These techniques require more heat and time to effectively draw out the beneficial compounds from these more robust plant parts.

Decoctions

Decoctions are suitable for extracting the properties of hard plant materials like roots and bark. This method involves simmering the herbs for an extended period to break down the tough plant cell walls.

Preparation Steps:

Measure Herbs: Use about one tablespoon of dried herbs per two cups of water.

Boil: Place the herbs in a pot with water and bring it to a boil.

Simmer: Reduce the heat and simmer the mixture for 20-30 minutes to allow the herbs to release their medicinal properties.

Strain and Use: After simmering, strain the liquid using a fine mesh strainer or cheesecloth. The decoction is now ready to be consumed or used for other purposes.

Use Case Example

Ginger Decoction: This decoction helps relieve muscle pain and inflammation, and can also soothe digestive issues. Ginger decoctions are often used in traditional medicine to treat colds and improve circulation.

Fomentations

Fomentations involve soaking a cloth in a hot herbal infusion or decoction and applying it to the affected area. This method is often used to treat external ailments such as muscle pain, skin conditions, or inflammation. The warmth of the compress helps to relax muscles, increase blood circulation, and enhance the absorption of the herbal properties. Additionally, it can be a soothing remedy for joint stiffness or respiratory issues when applied to the chest or back.

Preparation Steps:

Make a strong herbal infusion or decoction, depending on the desired strength and properties needed.

Soak Cloth: Soak a clean cloth in the hot liquid, ensuring it is fully saturated.

Wring Out Excess: Wring out the excess liquid to avoid dripping.

Apply: Apply the warm, damp cloth to the affected area. Cover with a dry towel to retain heat, if desired. Leave in place for 15-20 minutes.

Repeat as Needed: Re-soak and reapply the cloth as needed to maintain warmth and effectiveness.

Use Case Example

Arnica Fomentation: This fomentation helps reduce bruising, muscle pain, and inflammation. Arnica is known for its anti-inflammatory and pain-relieving properties, making it effective for treating sprains, strains, and muscle soreness.

Herbal Juices, Oils, and Ointments

Herbal preparations can take various forms beyond teas, such as juices, oils, and ointments, to provide therapeutic benefits. These methods allow the medicinal properties of herbs to be applied topically or consumed in concentrated forms, addressing a range of health concerns.

Herbal Juices

Herbal juices are made from fresh herbs and are typically consumed immediately to benefit from their potent, fresh properties.

Preparation Steps:

Select Fresh Herbs: Choose fresh, organic herbs. Wash them thoroughly to remove any dirt or contaminants.

Crush Herbs: Using a mortar and pestle or a blender, crush or blend the herbs to release their juice.

Strain Juice: Strain the crushed herbs through a fine mesh strainer or cheesecloth.

Consume Immediately: Drink the juice immediately to maximize its nutritional and medicinal benefits.

Use Case Example

Wheatgrass Juice: Consuming wheatgrass juice can help detoxify the liver, improve digestion, and boost energy levels. It's packed with vitamins, minerals, and antioxidants.

Herbal Oils

Herbal oils are created by infusing herbs in a carrier oil, allowing the oil to absorb the herb's properties. These oils can be used for massage, skin care, or medicinal purposes.

Preparation Steps:

Select Herbs and Carrier Oil: Choose fresh or dried herbs and a carrier oil such as olive, coconut, or almond oil.

Prepare Infusion: Fill a jar with the herbs and cover them with the carrier oil, ensuring the herbs are fully submerged.

Infuse: Let the mixture sit in a warm place for several weeks, shaking the jar occasionally to help the infusion process.

Strain and Store: After several weeks, strain the herbs out of the oil using a fine mesh strainer or cheesecloth. Store the herbal oil in a dark, cool place.

Use Case Example

Lavender Oil: Lavender-infused oil can be used for massages to relax muscles and reduce stress. It also soothes skin irritations and promotes healing of minor cuts and burns. Lavender oil is also known to improve sleep quality, making it a popular choice for nighttime relaxation rituals..

Herbal Ointments

Herbal ointments provide a protective barrier on the skin, allowing the healing properties of the herbs to penetrate deeply and effectively. They are especially beneficial for soothing dry, cracked skin and promoting faster recovery from cuts, burns, and rashes.

Prepare Herbal Oil: Follow the steps for creating herbal oil.

Melt Beeswax: In a double boiler, melt beeswax. Use about one ounce of beeswax per eight ounces of herbal oil.

Combine Oil and Beeswax: Once the beeswax is melted, slowly add the herbal oil to the double boiler, stirring constantly until fully combined.

Pour and Cool: Pour the mixture into containers and let it cool and solidify before using.

Use Case Example

Calendula Ointment: Calendula ointment helps heal cuts, burns, and skin irritations. It is often used to soothe eczema and rashes due to its gentle and healing nature. Calendula ointment can also reduce swelling and promote faster healing of minor wounds and abrasions.

This table covers a summary of the variety of ways to use teas and tisanes for medicinal purposes, including internal and external applications, along with examples for each method.

Method	Description	Application Area
Infusion	Steeping herbs in hot water to extract medicinal properties.	Internal use: digestion, respiratory support.
Decoction	Simmering tougher plant materials like roots and bark in water for extended time.	Internal use: muscle pain, inflammation, cold relief.
Cold Infusion	Steeping herbs in cold water for an extended period to extract properties.	Internal use: cooling and refreshing beverage.
Fomentation	Soaking a cloth in hot herbal infusion/decoction and applying it externally.	External use: muscle pain, skin conditions, inflammation.
Herbal Juice	Fresh herbs are crushed to release juice, consumed immediately for potency.	Internal use: detoxification, energy boost, nutrient intake.
Herbal Oil	Infusing herbs in carrier oil to absorb medicinal properties, used topically.	External use: massage, skin care, healing minor wounds.
Herbal Ointment	Mixing herbal oils with beeswax to create a thick preparation for topical use.	External use: treating skin conditions, minor wounds.

Table 1.7 ~ Ways to use teas and tisanes for medicinal purposes

Cautions in Preparing Herbal Remedies

When preparing herbal juices, oils, and ointments, it is essential to use high-quality, fresh ingredients and clean equipment. Always opt for organic herbs to avoid pesticides and contaminants. Use filtered or spring water to wash herbs and ensure carrier oils are pure and unrefined. Maintain proper proportions of herbs to oil or beeswax to achieve the desired consistency and effectiveness.

Store preparations in dark, cool places to extend their shelf life and preserve their properties. Always perform a patch test before using any new herbal preparation on the skin to check for allergic reactions. Consult a healthcare professional for any serious health conditions or if you are pregnant or nursing.

Panchamahabhutas: The Five Elements in Ayurveda

Ayurveda, the ancient system of medicine originating from India, is deeply rooted in the concept of the five elements, known as "Panchamahabhutas." These elements are **earth (Prithvi), water (Jala), fire (Agni), air (Vayu), and ether (Akasha)**. According to Ayurvedic philosophy, these five elements form the fundamental foundation of all matter in the universe and are present in varying degrees within all living and nonliving things. They are not only the building blocks of the natural world but also the essential components of the human body and mind.

These elements influence every aspect of our physical, mental, and emotional health, playing a crucial role in maintaining balance and harmony within the body according to Ayurvedic principles. After we explore the concept of the five elements, we will delve into how Ayurvedic teas can help balance the doshas that arise from imbalances in these elements. These teas are carefully crafted to restore harmony within the body and mind, supporting overall well-being.

Image 4.0~ Panchamahabhoota, the five elements of nature

Earth (Prithvi)

The earth element represents stability, structure, and solidity. It is associated with qualities such as heaviness, density, and groundedness. In the human body, the earth element is responsible for the formation of bones, muscles, tissues, and organs. It provides strength, endurance, and stability to the body.

Physical Impact: The earth element primarily affects the skeletal system, muscles, and tissues. It is responsible for the formation and maintenance of bones and the overall structure of the body.

Mental Impact: On a mental level, the earth element contributes to feelings of stability, groundedness, and security. It helps in building mental resilience and emotional steadiness.

Water (Jala)

The water element represents fluidity, cohesion, and adaptability. It is associated with qualities such as coolness, softness, and lubrication. In the human body, the water element is responsible for bodily fluids, including blood, lymph, mucus, and digestive juices.

It helps maintain hydration and supports smooth functioning of various systems.

Physical Impact: The water element primarily affects the circulatory system, digestive system, and tissues. It is responsible for the maintenance and transportation of bodily fluids and the hydration of tissues.

Mental Impact: On a mental level, the water element contributes to emotions and creativity. It helps in developing flexibility, adaptability, and a nurturing attitude.

Fire (Agni)

The fire element represents transformation, digestion, and metabolism. It is associated with qualities such as heat, intensity, and light. In the human body, the fire element is responsible for the digestive system, metabolism, and body temperature regulation. It helps in the conversion of food into energy and supports cognitive functions.

Physical Impact: The fire element primarily affects the digestive system, metabolic processes, and body temperature. It is responsible for the breakdown and assimilation of food and the regulation of metabolic rate.

Mental Impact: On a mental level, the fire element contributes to intelligence, clarity, and ambition. It helps in developing focus, determination, and the ability to perceive and understand.

Air (Vayu)

The air element represents movement, circulation, and respiration. It is associated with qualities such as lightness, dryness, and mobility. In the human body, the air element is responsible for the respiratory system, nervous system, and movement of muscles and joints. It supports circulation, respiration, and the transmission of nerve impulses.

Physical Impact: The air element primarily affects the respiratory system, nervous system, and joints. It is responsible for breathing, circulation, and the movement of muscles and joints.

Mental Impact: On a mental level, the air element contributes to creativity, flexibility, and communication. It helps in developing mental agility, adaptability, and the ability to express thoughts and ideas.

Ether (Akasha)

The ether element represents space, expansiveness, and connectivity. It is associated with qualities such as subtlety, lightness, and openness. In the human body, the ether element is responsible for cavities, channels, and spaces. It provides the space necessary for the movement and functioning of all other elements.

Physical Impact: The ether element primarily affects the cavities and spaces within the body, such as the mouth, nostrils, respiratory tract, and digestive tract. It provides the space necessary for the functioning of organs and systems.

Mental Impact: On a mental level, the ether element contributes to intuition, consciousness, and spiritual awareness. It helps in developing a sense of connection, openness, and expansiveness. Here is a brief overview of the five elements and how they influence the human mind and body.

Element	Primary Impact on the Body	Primary Impact on the Mind
Earth	Bones, muscles, tissues, organs (Skeletal and muscular systems)	Stability, resilience, groundedness
Water	Bodily fluids (circulatory and digestive systems)	Emotions, creativity, adaptability
Fire	Digestion, metabolism, body temperature (digestive system)	Intelligence, clarity, ambition
Air	Respiration, circulation, movement (respiratory and nervous systems, joints)	Creativity, flexibility, communication
Ether	Cavities, channels, spaces (all systems)	Intuition, consciousness, spiritual awareness

Table 1.8 ~ Elements (Panchamahabhuta) and Their Impact on the Human Body

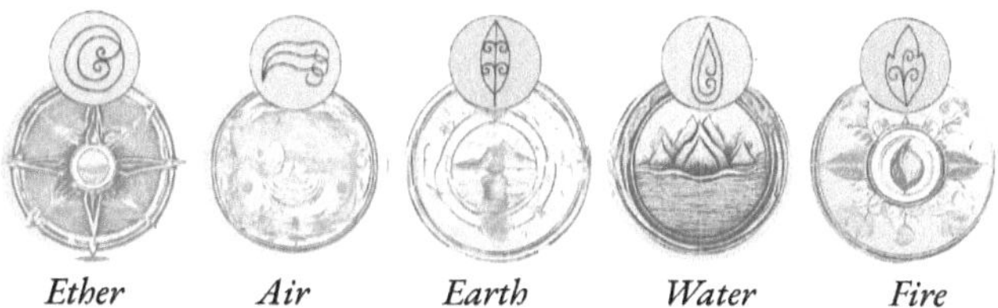

Image 4.1 ~Five Elements of Nature Described in Ayurveda

Understanding the five elements and their influence on the body and mind is essential for achieving balance and health. Each element has specific qualities and impacts, and their interactions within the body shape our physical and mental well-being. By recognizing these elements' roles, we can tailor our lifestyle, diet, and therapies to maintain harmony and address imbalances.

Tridosha: The Three Doshas and Body Types

The concept of the three doshas—Vata, Pitta, and Kapha—is fundamental to understanding individual constitution and health. As we know that these doshas are derived from the five elements and represent the three primary functional energies in the body. Each person has a unique combination of these doshas, which influences their physical, mental, and emotional characteristics.

वातः पित्तं कफश्चेति त्रयो दोषाः समासतः। विकृतिः स्थूलसंघातो मलानां सञ्चयस्तथा॥

Vata, Pitta, and Kapha are the three doshas, succinctly. They cause disease when in excess and balance when in harmony.

(Ether+Earth = Vata) - (Water+Fire = Pitta) - (Water + Earth = Kapha)

Image 4.2 ~Three Humors (Dosha) of body

Vata Dosha

Vata dosha is associated with the elements of air and ether. It governs movement, including circulation, respiration, and the nervous system. Vata is responsible for all bodily functions involving motion and flow.

Physical Impact: Vata controls bodily functions such as breathing, blinking, muscle and tissue movement, heartbeat, and cellular processes. It also influences the elimination of waste and the flow of thoughts in the mind.

Mental Impact: Vata governs creativity, flexibility, and communication. When balanced, it contributes to energy, enthusiasm, and adaptability. When imbalanced, it can lead to anxiety, fear, and restlessness.

Pitta Dosha

Pitta dosha is associated with the elements of fire and water. It governs digestion, metabolism, and energy production. Pitta is responsible for the body's metabolic processes and the transformation of nutrients into energy.

Physical Impact: Pitta controls digestion, absorption, assimilation, and body temperature. It also influences vision, skin complexion, and the metabolic rate.

Mental Impact: Pitta governs intelligence, focus, and determination. When balanced, it contributes to a sharp mind, leadership qualities, and clarity. When imbalanced, it can lead to irritability, anger, and inflammation.

Kapha Dosha

Kapha dosha is associated with the elements of earth and water. It governs structure, stability, and fluid balance in the body. Kapha is responsible for growth, lubrication, and the maintenance of bodily tissues.n.

Physical Impact: Kapha controls the formation and structure of bones, muscles, and tissues. It also influences the immune system, joint lubrication, and body fluid balance.

Mental Impact: Kapha governs calmness, stability, and compassion. When balanced, it contributes to patience, strength, and a sense of grounding. When imbalanced, it can lead to lethargy, attachment, and congestion.

Doshas and Their Impact on Body Type and Characteristics:

Characteristics	Vata	Pitta	Kapha
Body Type	Ectomorph	Mesomorph	Endomorph
Body Frame	Light, slender, delicate	Medium, muscular, well-built	Heavy, sturdy, broad
Hair Type	Dry, brittle, thin	Fine, straight, oily	Thick, wavy, oily
Hair Color	Dark, black, brown	Light, reddish, blonde	Dark, black, brown
Skin Type	Dry, rough, cool	Warm, oily, sensitive	Smooth, oily, cool
Skin Color	Dark, ashy, brown	Fair, rosy, reddish	Pale, white, yellowish
Body Weight	Low, difficulty gaining	Moderate, stable	High, easily gains weight
Eyes	Small, active, dry	Medium, sharp, intense	Large, calm, moist
Appetite	Irregular, variable	Strong, sharp	Steady, slow
Sleep	Light, interrupted	Moderate, sound	Deep, heavy
Mental Traits	Creative, lively, anxious	Intelligent, focused, irritable	Calm, loving, slow
Emotional Traits	Quick to worry, changeable	Quick to anger, passionate	Calm, forgiving, possessive

Table 1.9 ~ Three Doshas and Their Impact on Body Type and Characteristics

Doshas, Health Issues, and Herbal Tisanes

The balance of the three doshas (Vata, Pitta, and Kapha) is crucial for maintaining health. Imbalances in these doshas can lead to various health issues. Ayurveda offers natural remedies, including herbal tisanes, to restore balance and promote well-being. Below is a brief overview of the doshas, the health issues associated with their imbalance, and herbal tisanes to address these imbalances.

Dosha	Health Issues	Balancing Herbs
Vata	Anxiety, insomnia, dry skin, constipation, joint pain, irregular menstrual cycles	Ashwagandha, ginger, licorice, fennel, cinnamon, cardamom, ajwain
Pitta	Acid reflux, inflammation, skin rashes, irritability, excessive hunger or thirst, ulcers	Chamomile, mint, cummin, coriander, fennel, rose petals
Kapha	Weight gain, lethargy, congestion, water retention, depression, sluggish digestion	Ginger, turmeric, black pepper, cardamom, clove, fenugreek seeds

Table 2.0 ~ Three Dosha, their health issues and balancing herbs

Understanding your dominant dosha(s) can help you make informed lifestyle choices to maintain balance and promote health. Each dosha requires different approaches in diet, exercise, and daily routines to stay balanced. For example, Vata types benefit from warmth, regularity, and grounding activities, while Pitta types need cooling, calming, and moderate activities. Kapha types thrive with stimulating, invigorating, and varied routines.

Incorporating Ayurvedic principles into your daily life goes beyond just addressing immediate imbalances; it fosters a holistic approach to long-term health and vitality. By consistently choosing the right foods, herbs, and practices that align with your dosha, you create an environment within your body that supports natural healing and resilience. Herbal tisanes, customized to your dosha, serve as a gentle yet powerful tool in this process, helping to soothe, energize, or balance your system as needed. Embracing this ancient wisdom allows you to cultivate a deeper connection with your body, promoting not just the absence of illness, but a vibrant state of wellness.

References:

Lad, Vasant. The Complete Book of Ayurvedic Home Remedies. Three Rivers Press, 1998.
Frawley, David. Ayurveda and the Mind: The Healing of Consciousness. Lotus Press, 1997.
Pole, Sebastian. Ayurvedic Medicine: The Principles of Traditional Practice. Singing Dragon, 2006

Vata Balancing Tea

Soothing | Calm | Relaxing

Introduction:

Vata Balancing Tea is a carefully crafted blend designed to bring tranquility and comfort to both the mind and body, especially for individuals with a predominant Vata dosha. This soothing tea is particularly beneficial for those dealing with symptoms like anxiety, insomnia, restlessness, and fatigue.

By calming the nervous system, it helps restore balance and ease. Best enjoyed during the colder seasons or in the evening, this tea provides the perfect way to relax, unwind, and find peace at the end of a long day.

Brewing Instructions:

Boil 250 ml of water in a tea kettle.

Crush ¼ teaspoon each of ginger, cardamom, cinnamon, and ajwain (carom seeds) and place them in a teapot.

Pour the boiling water into the teapot.

Cover and steep the tea for 10 minutes.

Strain and serve hot.

Optional: Add lemon and honey to taste.

Health Benefits:

Enhances mental alertness

Supports bodily functions

Aids in relieving insomnia

Boosts immunity

Provides a sense of exhilaration

Image 4.3 ~Formation of Vata Dosha by Ether & Air Elements

When to Have This Tea:

Enjoy this tea in the evening or before bedtime to help relax and calm the mind. It is also beneficial during the cold seasons to balance the Vata dosha.

Who Should Not Take This Tea:

Individuals with a predominant Pitta dosha or those experiencing heat-related conditions should avoid this tea, as the warming spices may aggravate their symptoms. Pregnant women and people with certain medical conditions should consult their healthcare provider before consuming this tea.

Pitta Balancing Tea

Cooling | Refreshing | Aromatic

Introduction:

Pitta Balancing Tea is thoughtfully designed to bring cooling and refreshing relief to both the body and mind, especially for those with a predominant Pitta dosha. This rejuvenating tea is perfect for individuals experiencing symptoms such as rashes, skin inflammations, heartburn, visual problems, baldness, and excessive body heat.

By soothing the internal fire, it helps to restore harmony and calmness. Best enjoyed during the warmer seasons or whenever you need to cool down and unwind, this tea offers a revitalizing way to balance the Pitta dosha and maintain inner peace.

Brewing Instructions:

Boil 250 ml of water in a tea kettle.

Crush ¼ teaspoon each of fennel, coriander, and cumin; add 1 teaspoon of dried rose petals and a pinch of peppermint to a teapot.

Pour the boiling water into the teapot.

Cover and steep the tea for 10 minutes.

Strain and serve hot.

Optional: Add lemon and honey to taste.

Health Benefits:

Enhances digestion and promotes appetite

Normalizes heart rate

Provides a cooling effect

Boosts intellect

When to Have This Tea:

Image 4.4 ~Formation of Pitta Dosha by Water & Fire Elements

Enjoy this tea during the day, especially in the afternoon or early evening, to help cool and refresh your body and mind. It is particularly beneficial during the warmer seasons to balance the Pitta dosha.

Who Should Not Take This Tea:

Individuals with a predominant Vata dosha or those experiencing cold-related conditions should avoid this tea, as the cooling spices may aggravate their symptoms. Pregnant women and people with certain medical conditions should consult their healthcare provider before consuming this tea.

Kapha Balancing Tea

Spicy | Stimulating | Warm

Introduction:

Kapha Balancing Tea is expertly crafted to stimulate and invigorate both the body and mind, making it particularly beneficial for those with a predominant Kapha dosha. This energizing tea is ideal for individuals experiencing symptoms such as sluggishness, congestion, and excess weight, helping to clear the heaviness and lethargy often associated with Kapha imbalances.

By gently awakening the senses and boosting metabolism, it supports a more active and vibrant lifestyle. Best enjoyed during the cooler seasons or in the morning, this tea serves as the perfect way to kickstart your day with warmth, vitality, and renewed energy.

Brewing Instructions:

Boil 250 ml of water in a tea kettle.

Crush ¼ teaspoon each of ginger, clove, black pepper, and fenugreek seeds; add 2-3 strands of saffron to a teapot.

Pour the boiling water into the teapot.

Cover and steep the tea for 10 minutes.

Strain and serve hot.

Optional: Add lemon and honey to taste.

Health Benefits:

Enhances muscular strength

Boosts vitality and stamina

Strengthens immunity

Supports healthy, normal joints

When to Have This Tea:

Image 4.5 ~Formation of Kapha Dosha by Earth & Water Elements

Enjoy this tea in the morning or early afternoon to help stimulate and energize your body and mind. It is particularly beneficial during the cooler seasons to balance the Kapha dosha.

Who Should Not Take This Tea:

Individuals with a predominant Pitta dosha or those experiencing heat-related conditions should avoid this tea, as the warming spices may aggravate their symptoms. Pregnant women and people with certain medical conditions should consult their healthcare provider before consuming this tea.

Wellness Teas for Modern Life

In today's fast-paced world, our modern lifestyles, filled with hectic schedules, the constant use of gadgets, and exposure to pollution, pose numerous health hazards. These factors often lead to stress, fatigue, and a host of other health issues.

Amidst this chaos, adopting healthy drink options, such as wellness teas, can be a simple yet effective way to support our overall well-being. Wellness teas are not only delicious but also packed with natural ingredients that offer a range of health benefits. They serve as both a tasty treat and a healthy alternative, helping to detoxify the body, boost the immune system, and promote relaxation and vitality. Incorporating these teas into our daily routine can provide a soothing respite from the demands of modern life, offering a moment of tranquility and nourishment amidst the hustle and bustle.

Detox and Cleanse: Purifying Infusions

Detox and cleanse infusions are meticulously crafted to assist the body in the elimination of toxins, thereby enhancing overall health and vitality. These purifying beverages are often infused with a blend of herbs, flowers, spices, and fruits renowned for their cleansing properties.

Commonly used ingredients include dandelion root, ginger, peppermint, lemongrass, hibiscus, turmeric, lemon, and berries, which together create detox teas that are not only delicious but also highly effective.

These natural components work in harmony to support liver function, enhance digestion, and expel impurities from the body. For example, dandelion root is traditionally used to stimulate bile production, aiding in liver detoxification, while peppermint helps to soothe the digestive system.

Additionally, ginger and turmeric, both known for their potent anti-inflammatory and antioxidant properties, play a crucial role in reducing oxidative stress and inflammation within the body (as highlighted in the Journal of Traditional and Complementary Medicine, 2017). Regular consumption of these detoxifying teas can be particularly advantageous for those seeking to rejuvenate their system, especially after periods of dietary indulgence or exposure to environmental pollutants.

However, it's essential to note that detox infusions are not suitable for everyone. Pregnant or nursing women, individuals with pre-existing medical conditions, or those taking certain medications should refrain from consuming detox drinks without first consulting a healthcare provider. T

he powerful effects of these ingredients, while beneficial, may pose risks to individuals with specific health concerns, underscoring the importance of professional guidance before integrating these teas into one's routine.

Detox Tea

Cleansing | Energetic | Warm

Introduction:

Detox Tea is meticulously crafted to support the body's natural cleansing processes and effectively remove accumulated toxins, offering a gentle yet powerful aid in purification. Drawing from the time-honored principles of Ayurveda, this tea assists in detoxification by targeting impurities such as Ama, Amavisha, and Garavisha, which can develop due to factors like environmental toxins, poor diet, or changing weather conditions. Ideal for individuals looking to incorporate a purifying boost into their daily routine, Detox Tea enhances the body's natural defenses and promotes overall vitality, balance, and well-being, making it a valuable addition to a healthy lifestyle.

Brewing Instructions:

Boil 1 liter of water in a tea kettle.

Add ¼ teaspoon each of cumin, coriander, and fennel seeds to the boiling water.

Continue boiling for 10 minutes.

Cover and steep for an additional 10 minutes.

Strain and serve hot.

Drink throughout the day as desired.

Health Benefits:

Improves digestion

Enhances metabolism

Strengthens immunity

Boosts energy

When to Have This Tea:

Enjoy this tea throughout the day to support your body's detoxification process and maintain energy levels. It is especially beneficial during seasonal changes or when feeling sluggish.

Who Should Not Take This Tea:

Individuals with conditions that may be aggravated by herbal spices or those with particular health concerns are strongly advised to consult with a healthcare provider before incorporating this tea into their routine. It's essential to seek professional guidance to ensure that the ingredients in this tea are appropriate for your unique health circumstances and won't interfere with any existing conditions or medications.

Overall Wellness Tea

Sweet | Sour | Bitter

Introduction:

Overall Wellness Tea leverages the potent benefits of Triphala, a highly esteemed Ayurvedic blend of three powerful dried fruits: amalaki, bibhitaki, and haritaki. This tea is carefully crafted to enhance overall health and longevity, serving as a versatile remedy for a wide range of ailments.

By incorporating this tea into your daily routine, you support your pursuit of holistic wellness and a balanced, healthy lifestyle. Regular consumption of this tea can become a cornerstone in your journey toward optimal health and well-being.

Brewing Instructions:

Boil 250 ml of water in a tea kettle.

Add ½ teaspoon of Triphala powder to the boiling water.

Continue boiling for 10 minutes.

Cover and steep for an additional 10 minutes.

Strain and serve hot.

Health Benefits:

Supports immune system and detoxification

Aids digestion and promotes bowel regularity

Enhances dental health

Relieves occasional bloating and gas

Helps maintain blood sugar levels within a healthy range

Supports eye health and the visual system

When to Have This Tea:

Enjoy this tea any time of the day to promote overall wellness and address various health concerns. It is particularly beneficial when incorporated into a daily routine for sustained health benefits.

Who Should Not Take This Tea:

Individuals with particular health conditions or sensitivities to the components of Triphala should seek advice from a healthcare provider before consuming this tea. It is crucial for those with specific medical concerns or sensitivities to consult with a healthcare professional prior to incorporating this tea into their routine.

Memory Booster Tea

Cool | Bitter | Sharp

Introduction:

Memory Booster Tea harnesses the power of potent herbs such as Brahmi (Bacopa) and Shankhpushpi, which have been traditionally utilized in Ayurveda to enhance cognitive functions and boost memory.

This carefully crafted tea is designed to invigorate the mind, alleviate anxiety, and promote restful sleep, making it an ideal choice for those seeking to support cognitive health and enhance mental performance. Regular consumption of this tea may contribute to sharper focus, improved memory retention, and overall mental clarity.

Brewing Instructions:

Boil 250 ml of water in a tea kettle.

Add ¼ teaspoon each of Brahmi and Shankhpushpi powder to the boiling water.

Continue boiling for 10 minutes.

Cover and steep for an additional 10 minutes.

Strain and serve hot.

Enjoy this tea before bed to promote good sleep.

Health Benefits:

Boosts concentration

Acts as a nervine and brain tonic

Helps in managing Alzheimer's disease

Aids in reducing insomnia

Promoting good sleep

When to Have This Tea:

Enjoy this tea before bedtime to support memory and cognitive function while promoting relaxation and good sleep. It is particularly beneficial for individuals experiencing forgetfulness, anxiety, or sleep disturbances.

Who Should Not Take This Tea:

Individuals with particular health concerns or sensitivities to Brahmi and Shankhpushpi should seek advice from a healthcare provider before incorporating this tea into their routine. Consulting a healthcare professional is essential for those with specific health conditions or sensitivities to Brahmi and Shankhpushpi before consuming this tea.

Women's Wellness Tea

Cool | Bitter | Sweet

Introduction:

Women's Wellness Tea is expertly crafted to cater to the intricate and unique needs of a woman's body. Grounded in the wisdom of Ayurvedic tradition, this tea blends the nourishing properties of Shatavari, cinnamon, and fennel to foster harmony and balance, especially throughout the different stages of a woman's life.

This tea is specifically formulated to alleviate menstrual discomfort, support healthy digestion, and provide relief from menopausal symptoms, ensuring overall well-being and comfort.

Brewing Instructions:

Boil 250 ml of water in a tea kettle.

Add ¼ teaspoon each of Shatavari and fennel seeds, and ¼ inch of a cinnamon stick to the boiling water.

Continue boiling for 10 minutes.

Cover and steep for an additional 10 minutes.

Strain and serve hot.

Health Benefits:

Promotes harmony and balance

Helps maintain heat regulation

Supports menstrual regularity

Promotes digestive health

Eases menopause temperature fluctuations

When to Have This Tea:

Enjoy this tea at any time of the day to support overall well-being and address specific female health concerns. It is particularly beneficial during menstrual cycles and menopause for its soothing and balancing effects.

Who Should Not Take This Tea:

Individuals with particular health conditions or sensitivities to Shatavari, cinnamon, or fennel are strongly advised to seek guidance from a healthcare provider before consuming this tea. Consulting with a healthcare professional is essential for those with specific health concerns or sensitivities to these ingredients before including this tea in their routine.

Men's Vitality Tea

Astringent | Bitter | Hot

Introduction:

Men's Vitality Tea is crafted to cater to the unique and comprehensive health needs of men, drawing from the time-honored practices of Ayurveda. Central to this blend is Ashwagandha, a renowned adaptogenic herb celebrated for its broad range of health benefits.

This tea is formulated to boost mental clarity, alleviate stress, and support overall physical vitality, making it an essential component of a balanced and health-conscious lifestyle. By incorporating this tea into your daily routine, you can enhance mental resilience, reduce the impacts of stress, and promote a healthier, more robust body.

Brewing Instructions:

Boil 250 ml of water in a tea kettle.

Add ¼ teaspoon of Ashwagandha powder to the boiling water.

Continue boiling for 10 minutes.

Cover and steep for an additional 10 minutes.

Strain and serve hot.

Health Benefits:

Reduces blood sugar levels

Alleviates symptoms of depression

Decreases stress and anxiety

Increases muscle mass and strength

Boosts testosterone and enhances fertility

When to Have This Tea:

Enjoy this tea at any time of the day to support overall well-being and address specific male health concerns. It is particularly beneficial for reducing stress, enhancing physical performance, and boosting mental clarity.

Who Should Not Take This Tea:

Individuals with specific health conditions or sensitivities to Ashwagandha should consult with a healthcare provider before consuming this tea. Additionally, those on medications or with underlying health concerns should exercise caution and consult their healthcare provider.

Heart Health Care Tea

Sweet | Astringent | Aromatic

Introduction:

Heart Care Tea is expertly formulated to support cardiovascular health and overall well-being, drawing from the rich tradition of Ayurvedic medicine. This tea combines the potent benefits of arjuna bark, cinnamon, cardamom, mulethi, and rose petals into a powerful heart tonic.

The carefully selected blend works synergistically to reduce stress and anxiety, rejuvenate heart function, and maintain healthy blood pressure and cholesterol levels. Additionally, it supports liver health, providing a comprehensive approach to nurturing and protecting your heart and overall cardiovascular system. Incorporating this tea into your daily routine can enhance heart health, promote calmness, and contribute to a balanced, vibrant lifestyle.

Brewing Instructions:

Boil 500 ml of water in a tea kettle.

Add ¼ teaspoon each of arjuna bark powder, cinnamon, cardamom, and mulethi.

Add 1 teaspoon of rose petals to the boiling water.

Continue boiling for 10 minutes.

Cover and steep for an additional 10 minutes.

Strain and serve hot.

Health Benefits:

Reduces stress and anxiety

Rejuvenates heart function

Maintains healthy blood pressure and cholesterol levels

Supports liver health

When to Have This Tea:

Enjoy this tea at any time of the day to support cardiovascular health and overall well-being. It is particularly beneficial during times of stress or when seeking to maintain a healthy heart and liver.

Who Should Not Take This Tea:

Individuals with specific health conditions or sensitivities to any of the ingredients should consult with a healthcare provider before consuming this tea.

Digestive Harmony Tea

Warm | Spicy | Soothing

Introduction:

Digestive Harmony Tea is expertly crafted to support and soothe the digestive system, drawing upon the time-tested wisdom of Ayurvedic medicine. This blend features the synergistic benefits of ginger, fennel, and peppermint, which work together to promote healthy digestion, reduce bloating, and alleviate digestive discomfort.

The ginger aids in stimulating digestive enzymes, fennel helps to ease bloating and gas, while peppermint soothes the digestive tract and relieves symptoms of indigestion. Ideal for enjoying after meals or whenever you need a digestive boost, this tea provides gentle, effective support to maintain digestive health and comfort. Incorporating Digestive Harmony Tea into your routine can enhance overall digestive function and contribute to a more balanced, comfortable digestive experience.

Brewing Instructions:

Boil 250 ml of water in a tea kettle.

Add ¼ teaspoon each of crushed ginger and fennel seeds, and 1 teaspoon of dried peppermint leaves to the boiling water.

Continue boiling for 5 minutes.

Cover and steep for an additional 5 minutes.

Strain and serve hot.

Health Benefits:

Promotes healthy digestion

Reduces bloating and gas

Alleviates digestive discomfort

Soothes the stomach

When to Have This Tea:

Enjoy this tea after meals or whenever you experience digestive discomfort. It is particularly beneficial for easing bloating and supporting overall digestive health.

Who Should Not Take This Tea:

Individuals with specific health conditions or sensitivities to any of the ingredients, such as ginger, fennel, or peppermint, should consult with a healthcare provider before consuming this tea. This precaution helps ensure that the tea is suitable for your unique health needs and does not interfere with any existing medical conditions or treatments.

Anti-Inflammatory Tea

Spicy | Earthy | Warm

Introduction:

Anti-Inflammatory Tea is designed to help reduce inflammation in the body, promoting overall health and well-being. Rooted in Ayurvedic wisdom, this tea combines the powerful anti-inflammatory properties of turmeric, ginger, and black pepper to create a soothing and effective blend.

Regular enjoyment of this tea can support your body's natural defenses against inflammation, helping to alleviate discomfort and maintain balance. Ideal for those seeking relief from inflammatory conditions or wanting to enhance overall vitality, this tea serves as a natural ally in your wellness journey.

Brewing Instructions:

Boil 250 ml of water in a tea kettle.

Add ¼ teaspoon each of turmeric powder and crushed ginger, and a pinch of black pepper to the boiling water.

Continue boiling for 10 minutes.

Cover and steep for an additional 10 minutes.

Strain and serve hot.

Optional: Add a teaspoon of honey and a slice of lemon for added flavor and benefits.

Health Benefits:

Reduces inflammation

Boosts immune system

Aids in digestion

Supports joint health

When to Have This Tea:

Enjoy this tea at any time of the day to help reduce inflammation and support overall well-being. It is particularly beneficial after meals or during periods of increased physical activity.

Who Should Not Take This Tea:

Individuals with specific health conditions or sensitivities to any of the ingredients should consult with a healthcare provider before consuming this tea. Additionally, those taking medications or undergoing treatment for inflammatory conditions should seek professional advice to ensure compatibility and safety.

Weight Loss Tea

Bitter | Pungent | Spicy

Introduction:

Weight Loss Tea is crafted to support weight management by enhancing digestion and metabolism. Rooted in Ayurvedic wisdom, this tea combines the powerful properties of turmeric, ginger, black pepper, cinnamon, and peppermint. These ingredients work together to cleanse the body, boost metabolism, and promote overall digestive health. Regular consumption of this tea, alongside a balanced diet and exercise, may aid in achieving weight management goals.

Brewing Instructions:

Boil 1 liter of water in a tea kettle.

Add ½ teaspoon of fresh turmeric paste, ½ teaspoon of fresh ginger paste, 5-6 crushed black peppercorns, ½ inch cinnamon stick, and 1 teaspoon of fresh peppermint leaves to the boiling water.

Continue boiling for 10 minutes.

Cover and steep for an additional 10 minutes.

Strain and serve hot.

Optional: Add honey and lemon to improve the taste.

Keep drinking throughout the day while hot.

Health Benefits:

Increases bile production

Regulates blood sugar levels

Enhances metabolism

Strengthens immunity

Reduces inflammation

When to Have This Tea:

Enjoy this tea throughout the day to support weight management and enhance metabolism. It is particularly beneficial when consumed regularly to promote digestive health and cleanse the body of toxins.

Who Should Not Take This Tea:

Individuals with specific health conditions or sensitivities to any of the ingredients should consult with a healthcare provider before consuming this tea.

Anti-Allergic Tea

Soothing | Herbal | Mild

Introduction:

Anti-Allergic Tea is formulated to help alleviate allergy symptoms and support respiratory health with a robust blend of soothing and anti-inflammatory herbs. Combining the benefits of tulsi (holy basil), licorice root, ginger, fennel, chamomile, angelica, and yerba mate, this tea is designed to reduce inflammation, support the immune system, and ease respiratory discomfort.

Brewing Instructions:

Boil 500 ml of water in a tea kettle.

Add ¼ teaspoon each of dried tulsi leaves, licorice root, fennel seeds, and ¼ teaspoon of freshly grated ginger.

Add 1 teaspoon of dried chamomile flowers, ¼ teaspoon of dried angelica root, and 1 teaspoon of yerba mate leaves.

Continue boiling for 10 minutes.

Cover and steep for an additional 10 minutes.

Strain and serve hot. Add honey and lemon for added flavor.

Health Benefits:

Reduces allergy symptoms

Supports respiratory health

Soothes inflammation

Enhances immune function

Relieves congestion and promotes digestion

Provides mild energy boost and mental clarity (thanks to yerba mate)

When to Have This Tea:

Enjoy this tea when experiencing allergy symptoms or as a preventive measure to support respiratory health and reduce inflammation. It is particularly useful during allergy season or when exposed to environmental allergens.

Who Should Not Take This Tea:

Individuals with specific health conditions, sensitivities to any of the ingredients, or those on certain medications should consult with a healthcare provider before consuming this tea. Pregnant women and those sensitive to stimulants should use yerba mate cautiously.

More Purifying Infusions:

This table highlights a range of major health conditions beyond those addressed by the previously mentioned teas. It includes a curated list of beneficial herbs for each condition, along with the appropriate age groups for their use. This comprehensive guide offers insights into herbal remedies tailored to various health needs and life stages.

Health Condition	Beneficial Herbs	Age Group
Stress and Anxiety Relief	Ashwagandha, Holy Basil, Valerian Root, Lavender	Adults, Elderly
Enhancement of Skin Health	Red Clover, Turmeric, Holy Basil, Rose Petals, Calendula	All Ages
Uterine Health and Toning	Raspberry Leaf, Dong Quai, Shatavari	Women
Support for Bone Health	Turmeric, Nettle Leaf, Horsetail	Elderly
Relief from Joint Pain	Turmeric, Ginger, Devil's Claw, Boswellia, Celery Seed	Elderly, Adults
Increased Energy and Vitality	Ginseng, Ashwagandha, Rhodiola	All Ages
Support for Respiratory Health	Eucalyptus, Peppermint, Licorice Root, Tulsi	All Ages
Relief from Gas and Bloating	Fennel, Ginger, Peppermint, Cumin	All Ages
Management of Fever	Feverfew, Ginger, Peppermint, Tulsi	All Ages
Blood Purification	Turmeric, Burdock Root, Dandelion, Red Clover	All Ages
Relief from Cold and Flu Symptoms	Echinacea, Ginger, Elderberry, Peppermint, Honey	All Ages
Constipation Relief	Senna, Psyllium Husk, Fennel, Ginger	All Ages
Gout Management	Celery Seed, Turmeric, Ginger, Nettle Leaf	All Ages
Insomnia Relief	Valerian Root, Chamomile, Lavender, Ashwagandha	Adults, Elderly
Migraine Relief	Feverfew, Peppermint, Lavender, Ginger	Adults, Elderly
Motion Sickness Relief	Ginger, Peppermint, Fennel, Cardamom	All Ages
Hair Health Support	Rosemary, Nettle Leaf, Fenugreek, Amla	All Ages

Table 2.1 : List of various health conditions and beneficial herbs

A Friendly Note

I believe there's something truly special about the simple, wholesome remedies that have been passed down through generations. There's no doubt that knowing these home remedies is a wonderful way to care for yourself and your loved ones. After all, who doesn't love a good cup of tea that soothes the soul and nourishes the body? However, it's important to remember that while these remedies are a great addition to your wellness toolkit, they're not a replacement for professional medical advice or treatment.

If you're dealing with any serious health issues or considering making significant changes to your health routine, it's always wise to consult with your physician first. Think of these recipes as companions to your wellness journey, rather than a complete guide. Enjoy exploring them, but always keep your health expert in the loop. After all, taking care of yourself means knowing when to blend the old wisdom with modern expertise!

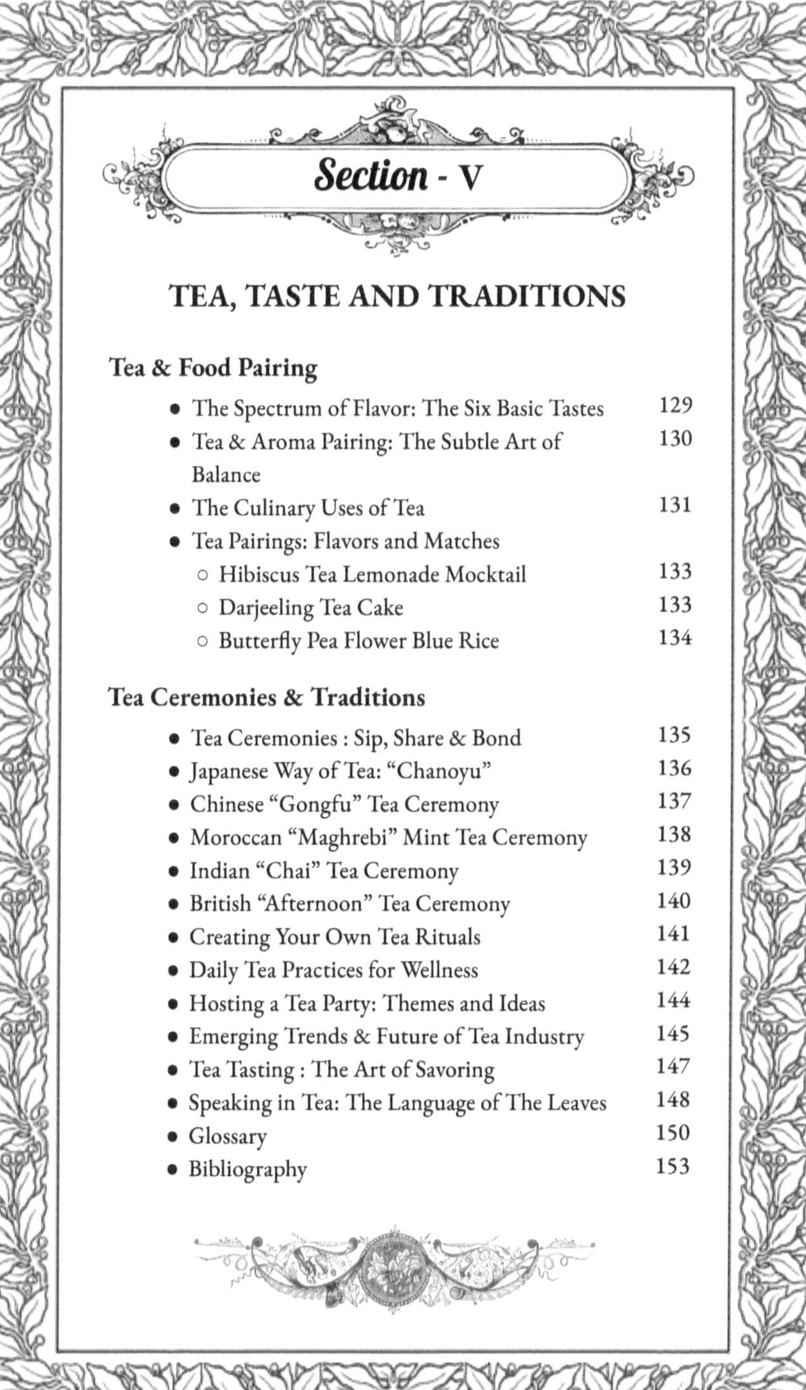

Section - V

TEA, TASTE AND TRADITIONS

TEAS AND TISANES : WHISPERS OF THE LEAF

"A quiet pause in the journey—just like letting the tea leaves settle."

1.7 - TEA GASTRONOMY: SWIRL OF FLAVOUR & AROMA

TEA & FOOD PAIRING

ea, with its rich history and cultural significance, transcends its role as a mere beverage. Its versatility extends to the culinary world, where it can enhance and complement a wide array of dishes. From savory marinades to sweet desserts, tea infuses a depth of flavor that elevates the dining experience

Just like wine, tea can be paired with food to elevate the dining experience, bringing out the best in both the tea and the dish. By understanding the balance between flavors and aromas, one can create harmonious combinations that delight the palate.

The Spectrum of Flavor: The Six Basic Tastes

Understanding the six basic tastes—sweet, salty, sour, bitter, umami, and pungent—provides a comprehensive approach to enhancing culinary experiences.

Each taste category brings its own unique character to food, and matching these with the right types of tea can create a harmonious balance that elevates both the tea and the dish. By exploring how different teas interact with these fundamental tastes, you can discover new dimensions of flavor and refine your palate.

> *"Tea, with its diverse range of aromas and flavors, offers endless possibilities for pairing with various taste profiles.*
>
> *Whether it's the subtlety of green tea balancing sweetness or the robust notes of black tea complementing umami, the key to perfect pairings lies in understanding how tea can enhance or contrast with the tastes present in your food.*
>
> *Dive into this guide to uncover how to match teas to each taste and elevate your culinary adventures".*

Sweet: Sweet foods are rich in sugar and are naturally pleasing to the palate. They can range from the simple sweetness of fruits to the complex flavors of desserts, often evoking comfort and indulgence.

Salty: Salty foods have a savory punch that enhances the flavors of other ingredients. This taste is prevalent in snacks, cured meats, and various savory dishes, creating balance and amplifying other tastes.

Sour: Sour foods have a tangy zest that adds a refreshing bite to dishes. This taste is found in citrus fruits, fermented foods, and some dairy products like yogurt, often stimulating the appetite and cleansing the palate.

Bitter: Bitter foods possess a sharp, sometimes challenging flavor that can add depth and complexity to dishes. Common bitter foods include dark chocolate, coffee, and certain vegetables like kale, which are often appreciated for their health benefits.

Umami: Umami, the savory taste, adds a rich, mouth-filling sensation to foods. It is often described as meaty or brothy and is found in foods like mushrooms, soy sauce, and aged cheeses, providing a deeply satisfying and lingering flavor.

Pungent: Pungent foods are known for their intense and spicy flavors. This taste is typically found in ingredients like chili peppers, garlic, and certain spices, often invigorating the senses and adding a fiery kick to dishes.

Tea & Aroma Pairing: The Subtle Art of Balance

The key to successful tea and food pairing lies in understanding the balance between flavors and aromas. The aromatic compounds in tea can either complement or contrast with the flavors of food, creating a harmonious balance that enhances the overall sensory experience. Different types of tea offer unique aromatic profiles that can be paired with various dishes to elevate their taste and aroma.

Black Tea with Rich Desserts: The robust, malty flavor of black tea pairs well with rich desserts like chocolate cake or brownies, providing a satisfying contrast that highlights the sweetness of the desert.

Green Tea with Light Salads: The delicate, grassy notes of green tea complement the fresh, crisp flavors of light salads, creating a refreshing balance that enhances the natural taste of vegetables.

Oolong Tea with Grilled Vegetables: The floral and fruity undertones of oolong tea enhance the smoky flavors of grilled vegetables, adding depth and complexity to the dish.

Pu-erh Tea with Aged Cheeses: The earthy, fermented notes of pu-erh tea complement the strong, salty flavors of aged cheeses, creating a complex and delightful combination that enhances both the tea and the cheese.

White Tea with Mild Cheeses : The gentle, nuanced flavor of white tea complements the creamy and slightly tangy notes of mild cheeses, creating a harmonious pairing that is both delicate and satisfying. This combination is perfect for a light snack.

Yellow Tea with Roasted Root Vegetables: The subtle, mellow sweetness of yellow tea pairs beautifully with the earthy and caramelized flavors of roasted root vegetables, creating a harmonious and balanced dish.

The Culinary Uses of Tea

Tea as a Flavoring Agent

Tea can be used to infuse subtle or bold flavors into a variety of dishes, adding a unique dimension that enhances the overall taste. By incorporating tea into cooking, one can create dishes that are both flavorful and healthful.

Soups and Stews:

Adding a sachet of green or black tea to soups and stews can impart a unique flavor profile that enhances the natural taste of the ingredients. For example, green tea can add a light, refreshing flavor to vegetable soup, while black tea can add depth and complexity to a hearty stew.

Sauces and Marinades:

Incorporating tea into sauces and marinades can add complexity and enhance the overall flavor of the dish. For instance, using Earl Grey tea in a marinade for tofu can add a citrusy, bergamot flavor that compliments the natural taste of the tofu.

Tea as a Smoking Ingredient:

Using tea leaves for smoking imparts a distinct aroma and flavor to a variety of foods, enhancing their taste and creating a unique sensory experience.

Tea-Smoked Tofu: Using green tea leaves to smoke tofu provides a delicate, herbal flavor that enhances the natural taste of the tofu. This method can also be used with other plant-based proteins, adding a unique dimension to the dish.

Tea-Smoked Vegetables: Smoking vegetables with black or oolong tea leaves imparts a rich, smoky flavor that enhances their natural taste, creating a delicious and healthful dish that can be enjoyed on its own or as a side.

Tea in Baked Goods and Desserts

Tea can add unique flavors and colors to a variety of baked goods and desserts, creating visually appealing and delicious treats that are both satisfying and healthful.

Matcha Cheesecake: The vibrant green color and earthy flavor of matcha make for a visually striking and delicious cheesecake that is both unique and healthful.

Earl Grey Cookies: The floral notes of Earl Grey tea add a sophisticated touch to traditional shortbread cookies, creating a delightful treat that is both elegant and flavorful.

Chai and Bun Maska, a quintessential treat at Irani cafes, marries the comforting warmth of spiced tea with the buttery softness of a fresh bun slathered in creamy butter, offering a simple yet nostalgic indulgence that captures the essence of Bombay's vibrant cafe culture.

Tea in Cocktails

Tea can be a versatile ingredient in both alcoholic and non-alcoholic cocktails, adding unique flavors and aromas that enhance the overall sensory experience.

Earl Grey Martini: Infusing gin with Earl Grey tea creates a sophisticated and refreshing cocktail that is both elegant and flavorful.

Green Tea Mojito: Combining green tea with mint and lime makes for a refreshing and healthful twist on the classic mojito.

Chamomile and Lavender Spritzer: Combining chamomile tea with lavender and sparkling water creates a calming and refreshing non-alcoholic beverage.

Tea Pairings: Flavors and Matches

Below is a table showcasing different types of tea and their compatible tastes:

Tea Type	Aroma Type	Taste Type	Pairing Food Type
Green Tea	Grassy, Fresh	Sweet, Sour, Umami	Pastries, Citrus Salads, Miso Soup
Oolong Tea	Floral, Fruity	Salty, Bitter, Umami	Nuts, Dark Chocolate, Roasted Vegetables
Black Tea	Malty, Robust	Salty, Umami, Pungent	Savory Snacks, Mushroom Risotto, Spicy Foods
Pu-erh Tea	Earthy, Rich	Salty, Bitter	Soy Sauce-Marinated Vegetables, Coffee Desserts
White Tea	Delicate, Subtle	Sour	Citrus Salads, Yogurt-Based Dishes
Herbal Tea	Sweet, Aromatic	Sweet, Bitter, Pungent	Fruit-Based Desserts, Dark Chocolate, Spicy Dishes
Floral Tea	Floral, Fragrant	Sweet, Bitter	Light Salads, Soft Cheeses, Fruit-Based Dishes
Fruit Tea	Fruity, Sweet	Sweet, Sour	Fresh Fruits, Yogurt-Based Desserts, Smoothies
Spice Tea	Spicy, Warm	Pungent, Bitter	Spicy Foods, Hearty Stews, Rich Desserts

Table 2.2 ~: Various type of teas, their aroma match, taste type and food pairing types

Tea's potential in the culinary world is vast and exciting. From enhancing flavors to providing a healthful component to dishes, tea offers endless possibilities for culinary innovation. Tea's versatility in cooking not only elevates traditional recipes but also inspires creative pairings and unique dishes that delight the palate.

Tea Infused Food and Drinks Recipes

Hibiscus Tea Lemonade Mocktail

Hibiscus tea lemonade is a refreshing and vibrant mocktail that combines the tartness of hibiscus with the zest of lemon. It's a perfect non-alcoholic drink for any occasion, offering a burst of flavor and a beautiful crimson color.

Ingredients:

2 cups water

2 tablespoons dried hibiscus flowers or 2 hibiscus tea bags

1/4 cup honey or sugar (adjust to taste)

1/4 cup freshly squeezed lemon juice

Lemon slices, for garnish

Ice cubes

Fresh mint leaves, for garnish

Instructions:

Boil the water and steep the hibiscus flowers or tea bags for 5-7 minutes until the water turns a deep red. Strain and let the tea cool. Sweeten with honey or sugar, then stir in the freshly squeezed lemon juice. Serve over ice, garnished with lemon slices and fresh mint leaves.

Darjeeling Tea Cake

Darjeeling tea cake is a delicate and aromatic dessert that incorporates the floral and fruity notes of Darjeeling tea. This cake is perfect for tea time or as a light dessert, offering a subtle yet sophisticated flavor.

Ingredients:

1 cup milk

2 tablespoons Darjeeling tea leaves or 2 Darjeeling tea bags

1 1/2 cups all-purpose flour, 1 1/2 teaspoons baking powder

1/2 teaspoon salt, 1/2 cup unsalted butter, softened

3/4 cup sugar, 2 large eggs

1 teaspoon vanilla extract.

Instructions:

Heat the milk until just boiling, then add the Darjeeling tea leaves or tea bags. Let it steep for 10 minutes, strain, and cool to room temperature. Preheat your oven to 350°F (175°C) and grease a loaf pan. In a bowl, mix the flour, baking powder, and salt. In another bowl, beat the butter and sugar until fluffy, then add the eggs one at a time, followed by the vanilla extract. Gradually add the dry ingredients, alternating with the cooled tea-infused milk, mixing until just combined. Pour the batter into the prepared pan and bake for 45-50 minutes, or until a toothpick inserted into the center comes out clean. Let the cake cool before slicing and serving.

Butterfly Pea Flower Blue Rice

Butterfly pea flower blue rice is a visually stunning and unique dish that brings a pop of natural blue color to your plate. The subtle, earthy flavor of the butterfly pea flowers pairs beautifully with the fragrant jasmine or basmati rice, making it an excellent accompaniment to various main courses.

Ingredients:

1 cup jasmine or basmati rice, 1 1/2 cups water

2 tablespoons dried butterfly pea flowers or 2 butterfly pea tea bags

1 tablespoon coconut oil or vegetable oil

1 small onion, finely chopped

2 cloves garlic, minced, Salt to taste, Fresh cilantro or parsley, for garnish

Instructions:

Begin by boiling the water and steeping the butterfly pea flowers or tea bags for 5-7 minutes until the water turns a vibrant blue. Strain and set aside. Rinse the rice under cold water until the water runs clear. Heat the oil in a pot over medium heat, then sauté the onion and garlic until translucent and fragrant, about 2-3 minutes. Add the rinsed rice to the pot, stirring to coat with oil. Pour in the blue tea, add salt to taste, and bring to a boil. Reduce the heat to low, cover, and simmer for 15-18 minutes until the rice is cooked and the liquid is absorbed. Remove from heat and let it sit covered for 5 minutes. Fluff the rice with a fork and garnish with fresh cilantro or parsley. Serve as a stunning side dish to curries, grilled vegetables, or any main course.

1.7 - TEA CEREMONIES & TRADITIONS

GLOBAL TEA CEREMONIES

ea ceremonies transcend the simple act of brewing and drinking tea; they are profound cultural rituals that encapsulate the values, traditions, and social customs of their respective regions. Tea ceremonies are performed in various ways across the world.

Each ceremony, with its unique set of practices and aesthetics, offers a window into the soul of a culture, showcasing a deep respect for tea and the art of its preparation.

SIP, SHARE & BOND

At the heart of tea ceremonies lies their extraordinary ability to create and nurture social bonds. These gatherings provide a tranquil, structured setting where individuals can unwind, converse, and connect on a deeper level. The ritual of sharing tea serves as a conduit for fostering relationships, promoting harmony, and encouraging mutual respect and understanding. It's in these serene moments that participants find joy and a sense of community, making tea ceremonies an unparalleled social activity.

Take, for example, the popular Indian tradition of "Chai par Charcha," where people meet over tea to discuss significant topics in a relaxed, informal setting. This practice highlights how tea can be a catalyst for meaningful conversation and camaraderie.

In Japan, the Chanoyu or tea ceremony is not just about the act of drinking tea but also about embracing aesthetics, manners, and the philosophical notion of 'Ichigo Ichie' – cherishing each encounter as a once-in-a-lifetime moment.

In these instances, tea becomes more than a beverage; it transforms into an experience that enriches social interactions. Whether it's the robust discussions over a cup of chai in India or the serene, meditative tea gatherings in Japan, tea ceremonies offer a unique blend of tradition, tranquility, and togetherness.

In the following pages, we will delve deeper into the fascinating world of tea ceremonies across different cultures. From the elegant Japanese Chanoyu to the vibrant Indian Chai tradition and the refined British Afternoon Tea, each ceremony brings its own unique flavor and cultural significance. Join us as we explore these enchanting rituals one by one, uncovering the stories and traditions that make each tea ceremony a cherished practice.

Japanese Way of Tea: "Chanoyu"

The Japanese Way of Tea, known as Chanoyu, is a ceremonial practice deeply rooted in Japanese culture, philosophy, and aesthetics. More than just the preparation and consumption of tea, Chanoyu embodies principles of harmony, respect, purity, and tranquility.

It has evolved over centuries, influenced by Zen Buddhism and the teachings of tea masters like Sen no Rikyū. This intricate ritual involves precise movements and a profound appreciation for the moment, the environment, and the company. Chanoyu is not only an art form but also a spiritual and meditative practice that fosters mindfulness and reverence for tradition.

Key Elements of the Chanoyu Tea Ceremony

Harmony (Wa): Emphasizes the balance and peaceful coexistence between host, guest, environment, and utensils.

Respect (Kei): Demonstrates reverence for others and for the tools and space used in the ceremony.

Purity (Sei): Focuses on cleanliness and simplicity, both physically and spiritually, to create a serene atmosphere.

Tranquility (Jaku): The ultimate goal, achieved through the mindful practice of the ceremony, leading to inner peace.

Tea Utensils: Includes chawan (tea bowl), chasen (bamboo whisk), chashaku (tea scoop), and natsume (tea caddy), each selected and handled with care.

Chaji: A full tea gathering, often encompassing a meal (kaiseki) and lasting several hours.

Seasonal Awareness: The selection of utensils, decor, and tea types are often chosen to reflect the current season.

Zen Influence: Chanoyu is deeply influenced by Zen Buddhism, encouraging mindfulness, simplicity, and presence in the moment.

Aesthetic Appreciation: Incorporates the Japanese concepts of wabi-sabi (beauty in imperfection) and ichi-go ichi-e (one time, one meeting).

Education and Practice: Learning Chanoyu involves years of study and practice, often under the guidance of a tea master.

Chanoyu is a testament to the Japanese appreciation for subtlety, precision, and the transient beauty of life, offering a unique and profound experience for both participants and observers. This revered tea ceremony embodies the art of mindfulness and harmony, creating moments of tranquility and reflection in a world often defined by its pace and distractions.

Chinese "Gongfu" Tea Ceremony

The Chinese Gongfu Tea Ceremony is an ancient and refined practice that embodies the essence of Chinese tea culture. Rooted in tradition and art, this ceremony is not just about drinking tea but appreciating its complex flavors, aromas, and the meditative process of preparation. "Gongfu" translates to "skill" or "effort," highlighting the precision and dedication required in this meticulous ritual.

Over centuries, this ceremony has evolved into a symbol of hospitality, respect, and mindfulness, offering a serene escape from the hurried pace of modern life.

Key Elements of the Gongfu Tea Ceremony

Tea Selection: High-quality, loose-leaf teas such as Oolong, Pu-erh, and green tea are preferred, chosen for their rich and complex flavors.

Teaware: The ceremony uses specialized teaware including a small teapot (Yixing clay or porcelain), a fairness cup, tea cups, and tea utensils like the tea scoop, tongs, and tea needle.

Water Quality and Temperature: Pure, clean water is essential, typically heated to the optimal temperature for the specific type of tea being brewed.

Warming and Rinsing: The teapot and cups are rinsed and warmed with hot water to ensure cleanliness and to enhance the tea's aroma and flavor.

Tea Brewing: Tea leaves are carefully measured and placed into the teapot. The first brew is often poured out to rinse the leaves, while subsequent brews are served to guests.

Pouring and Serving: Tea is poured into a fairness cup to ensure even flavor distribution, then served in small cups to guests, emphasizing sharing and hospitality.

Multiple Infusions: High-quality tea leaves can be brewed multiple times, with each infusion offering a different taste profile, allowing for a deeper appreciation of the tea's nuances.

Aromatic Appreciation: The ceremony involves appreciating the aroma of the tea, often by first smelling the lid of the teapot or the fairness cup before tasting.

Mindfulness and Respect: The entire process is conducted with mindfulness and respect, reflecting the harmony between nature, the tea, and the participants.

This beautiful and contemplative ceremony is a testament to the rich cultural heritage of China, providing a sensory journey that connects people and promotes a sense of well-being. Through its meticulous rituals and harmonious practices, it fosters a deeper appreciation for the art of tea and its role in nurturing both the body and spirit. This immersive experience not only celebrates tradition but also creates moments of tranquility and connection among participants.

Moroccan "Maghrebi" Mint Tea Ceremony

Moroccan Mint Tea is a cherished beverage and a symbol of hospitality, culture, and tradition in Morocco. This ritualistic drink, typically made from green tea, fresh mint leaves, and sugar, plays a crucial role in social gatherings and everyday life.

The preparation and serving of Moroccan Mint Tea is an art form passed down through generations, embodying the warmth and generosity of Moroccan people. It reflects the essence of Moroccan conviviality, offering a welcoming gesture that brings people together and celebrates the rich cultural heritage of the region.

Key Elements of the Moroccan Tea Ceremony

Cultural Significance: Moroccan Mint Tea is a symbol of hospitality and is often served to guests as a welcoming gesture. It reflects the host's respect and affection.

Ingredients: Moroccan Mint Tea is traditionally made with green tea, often Chinese gunpowder tea, which is known for its robust flavor. Fresh spearmint leaves are added to provide a refreshing herbal note, and a generous amount of sugar is incorporated to balance the flavors and enhance sweetness. This combination creates a harmonious blend that is both invigorating and satisfying.

Preparation: The brewing process of Moroccan Mint Tea is a distinctive and ceremonial ritual. It begins with steeping the green tea, followed by the addition of fresh mint leaves and a considerable amount of sugar. The tea is then poured from a height, a technique that not only develops a frothy head but also helps in blending the ingredients thoroughly. This method enhances the tea's flavor profile and imparts a unique texture, contributing to the overall sensory experience.

Serving Ritual: Traditionally served in small, intricately designed glasses, Moroccan Mint Tea is accompanied by sweet treats or snacks. The tea is poured in three distinct rounds, each offering a different flavor profile due to varying steeping times.

Social Aspect: The act of drinking Moroccan Mint Tea is a communal affair that promotes conversation and bonding. It plays a crucial role in social interactions, whether in private homes, bustling cafes, or during special celebrations.

Health Benefits: In addition to its cultural significance, Moroccan Mint Tea is valued for its digestive benefits and refreshing qualities, making it a beloved choice among locals and visitors alike.

Aesthetic Presentation: The tea is elegantly presented on a beautifully decorated silver tray, complete with a traditional teapot and ornate glasses, enriching the overall sensory experience and enhancing the ambiance.

Understanding and appreciating the Moroccan Mint Tea ritual provides a deeper insight into the rich cultural heritage and social customs of Morocco.

Indian "Chai" Tea Ceremony

Tea is more than just a beverage in India; it is a cultural experience deeply woven into the social and daily life of its people. The Indian way of drinking tea, known as "chai," is a ritual that brings together communities and families, symbolizing warmth, hospitality, and tradition. Unlike the formal tea ceremonies found in some other cultures, the Indian tea ceremony is informal yet rich with history and flavor.

It often involves a blend of strong black tea, milk, sugar, and an array of spices such as cardamom, ginger, and cloves, creating a unique and comforting drink.

Key Elements of the Indian Tea Ceremony

Chai Preparation Techniques:

Boiling Method: Black tea is boiled with water, milk, and spices.

Straining: The mixture is strained to remove tea leaves and spices before serving.

Ingredients Used:

Black Tea Leaves: The base of traditional chai.

Milk and Sugar: Added to create a creamy and sweet flavor.

Spices (Masala): Common spices include cardamom, ginger, cloves, and cinnamon.

Serving Style:

Small Glasses or Clay Cups (Kulhads): Tea is often served in small glasses or traditional clay cups, enhancing the aroma and taste.

Accompaniments: Commonly served with snacks like biscuits, samosas, or pakoras.

Social Aspect:

Community and Family: Chai is a social drink, often shared with guests, friends, and family.

Street Vendors (Chaiwalas): Popular in urban areas, where tea is prepared fresh and enjoyed on-the-go.

Time of Consumption:

Morning and Evening Ritual: Typically consumed in the morning and late afternoon or evening.

Breaks and Gatherings: Often enjoyed during work breaks or social gatherings.

The Indian tea ceremony is a celebration of flavor, community, and tradition, making chai an integral part of daily life in India. This cherished ritual brings people together, fostering connection and conversation over a cup of spiced tea. Each serving of chai reflects the warmth and hospitality that defines Indian culture.

British Afternoon Tea Ceremony

The British tradition of drinking tea, often referred to as "afternoon tea" or simply "tea time," is a quintessential aspect of British culture that dates back to the early 19th century. Originating with Anna, the Duchess of Bedford, this practice evolved into a sophisticated social ritual that has become synonymous with British identity. Tea time is not just about the beverage itself, but also about the etiquette, the accompaniments, and the setting, which together create an experience that is both relaxing and refined.

This cherished tradition embodies a blend of elegance and comfort, where the art of tea drinking is accompanied by an array of delicate finger sandwiches, scones with clotted cream and jam, and an assortment of pastries. The ritual of afternoon tea offers a delightful pause in the day, providing an opportunity for social interaction and leisurely conversation amidst the soothing ambiance of a well-set tea table. The ceremonial aspects of tea time, from the precise preparation of the tea to the careful arrangement of treats, reflect the British dedication to grace and hospitality, making it an enduring symbol of cultural heritage and refined taste.

Key Elements of British Tea Ceremony

Timing: Afternoon tea is typically served between 3:30 and 5 PM. It was originally intended to fill the long gap between lunch and dinner.

Types of Tea: Popular choices include Earl Grey, Darjeeling, Assam, and English Breakfast. Tea is usually served in fine china cups.

Tea Preparation: Loose tea leaves are often preferred over tea bags. The tea is steeped in a teapot, and hot water is added to the pot rather than to individual cups.

Milk First or Last: There is an age-old debate about whether milk should be added before or after pouring the tea. Traditionally, milk was added first to prevent the fine china from cracking under the heat.

Accompaniments: Typical accompaniments include finger sandwiches, scones with clotted cream and jam, and a variety of pastries and cakes.

Etiquette: Proper etiquette involves holding the cup by the handle, sipping quietly, and placing the cup back on the saucer between sips. Pinkies should not be extended.

Setting: The setting is often elegant, with a table laid out with a crisp white tablecloth, fine china, and silverware. Floral arrangements and tiered trays add to the ambiance.

Social Aspect: Tea time is a social event, providing an opportunity for conversation and relaxation. It is often enjoyed with friends and family.

This time-honored tradition continues to be a cherished part of British life, celebrated in homes, tea rooms, and hotels across the United Kingdom. It remains a beloved occasion that brings together friends and family, fostering a sense of community and offering a delightful escape from the everyday hustle.

Creating Your Own Tea Rituals

In the previous chapter, we explored the rich tapestry of global tea ceremonies, each with its unique traditions and cultural significance. Now, let's delve into how you can create your own meaningful tea rituals at home, blending these time-honored practices with personal touches to enhance your daily life.

Designing Your Tea Space

In our journey through the world of tea, we now turn inward, crafting a space within our homes where tranquility and mindfulness can flourish. This chapter isn't merely a guide—it's an invitation to create a sanctuary, a haven where the simple act of drinking tea becomes a cherished ritual.

Choosing the Right Location

The foundation of your tea sanctuary begins with selecting the perfect spot. Imagine a quiet corner of your home, away from the chaos of daily life, where you can retreat and find solace. Perhaps near a window where the gentle play of natural light can dance upon your teacup, casting a serene glow that invites you to unwind and savor each sip. This chosen location will be your personal escape, a place where the world fades away and peace envelops you.

Selecting Comfortable Furniture

Comfort is the soul of your tea ritual. Imageture yourself sinking into a plush armchair or resting upon a cushioned bench, where every contour supports good posture and enhances your tea-drinking experience. A small table by your side holds your teapot and cups, making the ritual both practical and delightful. As you settle in, feel the embrace of comfort wrapping around you, turning each tea session into a moment of pure indulgence.

Incorporating Aesthetic Elements

The aesthetics of your tea space are an extension of your soul. Let your personal style shine through, whether it's the clean lines of minimalism, the eclectic charm of bohemian decor, or the timeless elegance of traditional elements.

Imagine the vibrant green of potted plants bringing life to your space, or the delicate brushstrokes of artwork adorning your walls. A beautiful tea set, carefully chosen, becomes a centerpiece that reflects your unique taste. These elements weave together to create an inviting haven that is unmistakably yours.

Organizing Tea Accessories

In the heart of your tea sanctuary, organization brings a sense of harmony. Envision a stylish tea tray or a dedicated shelf where your teapots, cups, and other essentials are lovingly arranged. This thoughtful organization streamlines your tea ritual, making it seamless and enjoyable.

As you reach for your favorite teapot or a cherished cup, everything is within easy reach, ensuring that each tea session flows with effortless grace.

Enhancing Ambiance with Lighting and Sound

The ambiance of your tea space is the final touch, elevating it to a realm of tranquility. Soft, warm lighting from lamps or candles bathes the room in a gentle glow, creating an atmosphere of calm. Imagine the soft strains of background music or the soothing sounds of nature filling the air, each note enhancing your relaxation. These sensory elements envelop you, transforming your tea ritual into an immersive and restorative experience.

In crafting your tea space, you are not just creating a physical setting; you are weaving a tapestry of peace and joy, a retreat where the simple act of drinking tea becomes a profound journey of the soul. As you sit in your sanctuary, feel the weight of the world lift, replaced by the delicate beauty of the moment, where every sip of tea is a step towards inner tranquility.

Daily Tea Practices for Wellness

As we journey deeper into the world of tea, we discover that it is more than just a beverage—it is a pathway to wellness, a companion in our daily lives that can energize, focus, and calm us. Integrating tea into your daily routine can be a powerful practice, enhancing both your physical well-being and mental mindfulness. In this chapter, we explore how different teas can be woven into your day to create moments of health and tranquility.

Morning Energizing Tea

The dawn of a new day is a time of renewal and possibility, and beginning it with the right tea can set a positive and energizing tone. Imagine starting your morning with a cup of green tea or matcha, rich in antioxidants and moderate caffeine.

These teas not only boost your metabolism but provide sustained energy, steering clear of the harsh crash often associated with coffee. For example, a study published in the "American Journal of Clinical Nutrition" found that green tea extract can significantly increase fat oxidation during exercise, making it a perfect morning companion . As the steam rises from your cup, feel the gentle awakening of your senses, preparing you to embrace the day with vitality and clarity.

Afternoon Focus Tea

The afternoon often brings a natural dip in energy and focus, a common challenge known as the afternoon slump. Yet, the right tea can help maintain your productivity and alertness. Picture a steaming cup of oolong or yerba mate, known for their cognitive-enhancing properties. Research from "Phytomedicine" suggests that yerba mate can improve cognitive function and attention.

These teas help keep your mind sharp and your spirits high, enabling you to navigate the rest of your day with sustained concentration and vigor. As you sip, feel the rejuvenation flow through you, recharging your focus and determination.

Evening Relaxation Tea

As the sun sets and the day winds down, a calming tea can aid in relaxation and prepare you for a restful night. Envision yourself with a soothing cup of chamomile, lavender, or valerian root tea. These herbal infusions have natural sedative properties that help reduce anxiety and promote sleep. For instance, a study in "BMC Complementary and Alternative Medicine" highlighted that chamomile can significantly improve sleep quality among individuals suffering from insomnia . Let the gentle aroma and warmth of the tea envelop you, easing the tensions of the day and inviting a state of peace and tranquility. With each sip, you move closer to a serene and restful slumber.

Mindfulness and Tea Meditation

Incorporating mindfulness into your tea practice can profoundly enhance its benefits. Use your tea time as an opportunity for meditation, focusing intently on the sensations of brewing and drinking your tea.

Notice the warmth of the cup in your hands, the delicate aroma wafting through the air, the complex flavors unfolding on your palate. This mindful approach helps ground you in the present moment, transforming a simple tea ritual into a meditative and centering experience. For instance, the Zen Buddhist tea ceremony, known as "Chado" or "The Way of Tea," emphasizes the importance of mindfulness and presence, turning tea drinking into an art form . With each mindful sip, you cultivate a deeper connection to the here and now.

Incorporating Herbs for Health

The natural world offers a bounty of herbs, each with unique health benefits, and incorporating them into your tea can be a delightful way to boost wellness. For instance, ginger can aid digestion, while peppermint can relieve headaches. A study in "Journal of Pain" showed that peppermint oil is effective in reducing the intensity of headaches . Experiment with different herbal blends to discover what works best for your body and needs. As you explore these herbal infusions, you'll find a harmonious blend of flavors and health benefits, enhancing your daily tea rituals.

Integrating Tea for a Balanced Life

Incorporating these daily tea practices into your routine can transform ordinary moments into rituals of wellness and mindfulness. Whether it's the energizing start with a morning green tea, the focused afternoon with oolong, the calming embrace of evening chamomile, or the meditative pauses throughout the day, tea offers a simple yet profound way to enhance your well-being. As you make these practices your own, you'll find that each cup of tea becomes a moment of nourishment for both body and soul.

Hosting a Modern Tea Party: Themes and Ideas

A tea party is not merely an event; it is an art form, an elegant tapestry woven with threads of tradition, innovation, and personal touch. Hosting a modern tea party requires a delicate balance of these elements to craft an experience that resonates with your guests. Here's a guide to help you orchestrate a tea gathering that is both sophisticated and memorable.

Choosing a Theme

The theme of your tea party is the canvas upon which your vision is painted. It provides the foundation for decor, menu, and activities, ensuring that every detail harmonizes to create a cohesive experience. Consider themes that evoke charm and elegance, such as a serene garden tea party, a nostalgic vintage affair, or an adventurous international tea tasting. Each theme sets the stage for a unique atmosphere—whether it's the romance of a blooming garden, the allure of bygone eras, or the excitement of discovering global flavors. Choose a theme that reflects your personal style and interests, and let it guide every decision.

Curating a Tea Menu

At the heart of any tea party lies its menu—a delightful array of flavors and textures that tantalize the palate. Craft a menu that offers a diverse selection of teas to cater to varying preferences. Include classic black teas for traditionalists, refreshing green teas for the health-conscious, soothing herbal teas for those seeking relaxation, and exotic specialty blends for adventurous taste buds. Complement these brews with an assortment of finger foods: flaky scones with clotted cream, dainty sandwiches with savory fillings, and delicate pastries that beckon with their sweetness. Remember to consider dietary restrictions and provide options that accommodate all your guests.

Creating Invitations

The invitation sets the stage for your tea party, providing a glimpse into the elegance and anticipation of the event. Choose invitations that mirror your theme—whether through digital designs or traditional printed cards. Ensure that your invitations are both beautiful and informative, detailing the date, time, location, and any dress code or special instructions. An invitation that captures the essence of your gathering will spark excitement and set the tone for a delightful experience.

Setting Up the Space

Transform your space into a haven of charm and elegance. The setting should reflect your theme and create an inviting atmosphere for your guests. Use decorative elements like tablecloths adorned with floral patterns, fresh blooms arranged in vases, and an elegant tea set that adds a touch of sophistication. Arrange seating in a visually appealing and functional way to facilitate conversation and ensure there is ample space for guests to move comfortably.

Activities and Games

Infuse your tea party with engaging activities that enhance the theme and provide interactive fun. A tea tasting session can be an enlightening experience, allowing guests to sample various teas and learn about their unique characteristics. Incorporate traditional tea party games such as a tea trivia quiz to challenge and entertain your guests, or a best hat contest to add a touch of whimsy. These activities not only entertain but also educate, making your tea party a memorable and enriching event.

By thoughtfully curating each aspect of your tea party—from the chosen theme and menu to the invitations, setting, and activities—you create an occasion that celebrates the art of tea and the joy of shared moments. Embrace the nuances of tea culture and let your creativity shine through, crafting an experience that will linger in the hearts of your guests long after the last cup is sipped.

Emerging Trends & Future of Tea Industry

The tea industry is experiencing a renaissance, driven by a confluence of innovations and emerging trends that are reshaping how we grow, prepare, and enjoy this cherished beverage. This chapter explores the dynamic changes that are defining the future of tea, blending sustainability with technological advancements and evolving cultural influences.

Sustainability is at the forefront of modern tea farming, reflecting a growing awareness of environmental impacts and ethical considerations. Progressive tea estates like Nanda Estate in India are setting new standards with their organic farming methods and agroforestry practices. By integrating tree planting with tea cultivation, these estates are not only enhancing biodiversity but also improving soil health, setting a benchmark for responsible tea production. Fair trade initiatives, spearheaded by organizations such as the Ethical Tea Partnership, are also making significant strides. These efforts ensure that tea farmers receive fair wages and work under better conditions, aligning with the increasing consumer demand for ethically produced goods.

At the same time, technology is revolutionizing the tea experience. Smart brewing devices, exemplified by Breville's Smart Tea Infuser, are transforming how we prepare tea. These devices offer precise controls for temperature and brewing time, allowing tea enthusiasts to achieve the perfect brew every time. Similarly, iKettle's smart kettle, which connects to a smartphone app, adds a layer of convenience to tea-making by enabling users to set their preferred temperature and schedule boiling times. These technological advancements are making the tea preparation process more consistent and enjoyable, blending tradition with modern convenience.

The digital age has also expanded and enriched tea culture, creating a vibrant global community of enthusiasts. Social media platforms such as Instagram and YouTube are brimming with tea influencers and aficionados who share their experiences, recipes, and recommendations. Influencers like Lisa and Sarah from Tea Lovers have cultivated substantial followings, contributing to the global spread of tea culture through engaging content. Online communities, including Reddit's Tea Community, provide spaces for tea lovers to connect, discuss, and share, fostering an inclusive and accessible global network.

As the tea industry evolves, several emerging trends are shaping its future. Fermented teas, such as kombucha, have gained popularity for their unique flavors and health benefits. Pioneering brands like GT's Kombucha offer a range of probiotic-rich flavors that appeal to health-conscious consumers. Beyond kombucha, other fermented teas like pu-erh and jun are being explored for their distinctive taste profiles and potential health benefits, adding depth and variety to the tea market.

The fusion of tea with wellness trends is another significant development. Brands like Pukka Herbs are integrating wellness-focused ingredients into their tea blends, offering products designed for relaxation, detoxification, and energy boosts. The incorporation of CBD and other supplements into tea reflects a broader trend toward holistic health solutions, catering to consumers seeking comprehensive well-being support.

Tea tourism is also emerging as a unique and immersive travel experience. Destinations such as Hangzhou in China, Darjeeling in India, and Nuwara Eliya in Sri Lanka offer visitors the chance to explore tea plantations, participate in traditional tea ceremonies, and gain insights into the rich history of tea production. This trend invites tea enthusiasts to experience the origins and traditions of their favorite beverage firsthand, adding a new dimension to the appreciation of tea.

Tea Tasting : The Art of Savoring

Ah, dear reader, it seems we were parted for a time—left somewhere in the middle of these pages. But like a good cup of tea that's been set aside for a moment, I am here once more, warm and inviting, ready to continue our journey together. Let me guide you through the art of tea tasting, where my leaves, my aroma, my body, and my soul are revealed.

Visual Beginnings: My First Impression

As you first lay eyes on me, know that my appearance tells a story. My shape, color, and texture are the first clues to understanding my journey. When I'm fresh, I retain a resilience—you might press me gently, and I'll spring back, a sign of my vitality. If I've aged, however, I may crumble under your touch, revealing the passage of time. Take a moment to observe me; my leaves are the first whispers of what lies within.

Aromatics: Breathing in My Essence

Inhale deeply and let my scent envelop you. Before I've even touched water, my fragrance carries the secrets of my origin. Am I floral, fruity, or perhaps earthy?

These scents are not merely pleasant—they are the key to unlocking my character. As I steep, my aroma will evolve, growing richer and more complex. Breathe in my essence, for it is here that my spirit begins to speak.

Image 4.5 ~A Tea Sommelier

Taste: Savoring My Soul

Now comes the moment when I truly come alive in your cup. As you taste me, allow the liquid to dance across your palate. My flavors are many—sometimes sweet, sometimes bitter, sometimes a delicate balance of both. The tip of your tongue will catch my sweetness, while the back will sense my bitterness. As you swirl me in your mouth, you'll feel my body, my thickness, my texture. Each sip is a conversation between us, where I share the story of my creation, from the soil I grew in to the hands that shaped me.

Touch: Feeling My Texture

As I flow across your tongue, you'll notice my texture—am I smooth and full-bodied, or light and delicate? The viscosity of my liquor tells you much about my quality. When I am thick and full, I carry with me the richness of the earth. If I am light, I might bring a sense of airiness, a reflection of the high altitudes where I may have grown. Feel me as I glide, and you'll understand the care that has gone into making me who I am. My tale is one of transformation, from a simple leaf to a complex, nuanced cup of tea. Each step of tasting reveals another layer of my identity, and by the end, you'll know me as intimately as I know myself.

Speaking in Tea: The Language of The Leaves

If you listen closely, you'll hear me speak. Not in words, but in the unique language of tea—a language that has been shaped over centuries by those who have learned to understand me.

This chapter is my way of teaching you how to decipher the words I whisper, the terms that describe who I am in the most intricate detail.

Liquor: The Heartbeat of My Being

When I am brewed, I reveal my heart—my liquor. You'll see it in the color, feel it in the body, and taste it in every sip. My liquor might be "brisk," lively and invigorating, or perhaps "flat," if something in my journey has dulled my spirit. The color of my liquor, whether it is bright or deep, speaks of my strength and character.

Autumnal: If I carry this term, it means I was born in the autumn, my flavor rich and robust like the season itself.

Bright: When I'm bright, my liquor is clear, vibrant, full of life. It's a sign that I am fresh, ready to refresh your palate.

Malty: This is my warmth, my richness, often found in Assams. It's a deep, comforting note that lingers long after the sip.

Infused Leaf: My Afterglow

After you've brewed me, look at my infused leaves. They are what remains after I've shared my essence with you. Their color, texture, and aroma are still speaking—telling you how I was crafted, and whether I was treated with care.

Coppery: If my infused leaves shine with this color, know that I was well made, my quality assured.

Even: When my leaves are uniform, it shows I was carefully processed, with consistency that speaks of my quality.

Green: Sometimes, I might carry this color, a sign that my journey was cut short, that I was not fully allowed to become who I am meant to be.

Dry Leaf: My First Whisper

Before water ever touches me, my dry leaves are where you'll first hear my voice. Their appearance is my introduction, a sign of what's to come.

Bloom: When I have bloom, I am alive with freshness, my leaves bright and inviting, full of potential.

Stylish: If I am stylish, my leaves are neat, even, a sign of careful craftsmanship.

Whiskery: This term might hint at fibers that cling to me, not a flaw, but a part of my unique character.

Aroma and Flavor: My Final Song

As you bring me close, the aroma is the first note of my final song. My fragrance is complex, a bouquet of scents that tell you where I've been and what I've become.

Astringency: You'll feel this as a clean, refreshing sensation, a slight dryness that leaves your mouth wanting more.

Muscatel: If you find this, you're tasting the soul of Darjeeling, a flavor as rare and precious as the grapes it's named after.

Vegetal: This is my green side, a grassy freshness that reminds you of the gardens where I grew.

To know me is to learn my language. Every term, every note, is a part of my story, and through this book, I hope to teach you how to listen. As I bring my tale to a close, I want to express my deepest gratitude for the time you've spent with me. Each moment we've shared has been steeped in the rich aromas and delicate flavors of discovery.

Thank you for allowing me into your world, for savoring each sip, and for finding joy in my many forms. Though our time together in these pages ends here, I hope to meet you again—perhaps in the gentle steam of your morning cup or the quiet comfort of an evening brew.

"Until our paths cross again, my dear,

May each dawn whisper memories near.

In every cup, in every embrace,

Our love will linger, time cannot erase.

Till the morning sun warms our hearts anew,

Know that each day, I'll be waiting for you."

Assam Tea - Camellia sinensis - असम चाय

Assam Tea is known for its strong, malty flavor and dark color. It's a popular black tea variety from the Assam region in India, prized for its robust taste.

Black Tea - Camellia sinensis - काली चाय

Black Tea is fully oxidized, offering a bold and rich flavor profile. It is commonly enjoyed with milk or as a base for blends like Earl Grey.

Ceylon Breakfast - Camellia sinensis - श्रीलंकन ब्रेकफास्ट चाय

Ceylon Breakfast Tea is a robust black tea with a bright, brisk flavor from Sri Lanka. It is perfect for a strong morning brew.

Ceylon Tea - Camellia sinensis - श्रीलंका चाय

Ceylon Tea offers a bright, citrusy flavor with a golden hue. It's a black tea from Sri Lanka, known for its refreshing taste and aromatic quality.

China Rose Tea - Camellia sinensis with Rosa spp. - चीनी गुलाब की चाय

China Rose Tea blends black tea with rose petals, providing a fragrant and mildly sweet flavor. It combines the richness of tea with the delicate essence of roses.

Darjeeling Tea - Camellia sinensis - दार्जिलिंग चाय

Darjeeling Tea is often referred to as the "Champagne of Teas," known for its muscatel flavor and delicate aroma. It hails from the Darjeeling region in India.

Earl Grey Tea - Camellia sinensis - अर्ल ग्रे चाय

Earl Grey Tea is a black tea flavored with bergamot orange oil, giving it a distinctive citrus aroma and a sophisticated taste.

English Breakfast Tea - Camellia sinensis - इंग्लिश ब्रेकफास्ट चाय

English Breakfast Tea is a strong, full-bodied black tea blend traditionally enjoyed with breakfast. It's known for its robust flavor and high caffeine content.

Irish Breakfast Tea - Camellia sinensis - आयरिश ब्रेकफास्ट चाय

Irish Breakfast Tea is a rich and hearty black tea blend with a malty flavor. It's stronger than English Breakfast Tea and often enjoyed with a splash of milk.

Jasmine Tea - Camellia sinensis with Jasminum spp. - जैस्मिन चाय

Jasmine Tea combines green tea with jasmine blossoms, offering a sweet, floral aroma and a delicate, soothing taste.

Keemun Tea - Camellia sinensis - कीमुन चाय

Keemun Tea is a Chinese black tea with a fruity, slightly smoky flavor. It's renowned for its rich taste and complex aroma.

Lapsang Souchong Tea - Camellia sinensis - लैपसांग सौचौंग चाय

Lapsang Souchong is a black tea with a distinctive smoky flavor, achieved through traditional drying over pine fires.

Lemon Tea - Camellia sinensis with Citrus limon - नींबू चाय

Lemon Tea is made by infusing black tea with lemon, providing a refreshing and tangy flavor that's perfect for a revitalizing drink.

Ping Suey Tea - Camellia sinensis - पिंग सुय चाय

Ping Suey Tea is a light and aromatic tea with a subtle, delicate flavor, popular in Chinese tea culture.

Prince of Wales Tea - Camellia sinensis - प्रिंस ऑफ वेल्स चाय

Prince of Wales Tea is a black tea blend known for its smooth, full-bodied flavor and delicate aroma, historically associated with British royalty.

Russian Caravan Tea - Camellia sinensis - रूसी कारवां चाय

Russian Caravan Tea is a smoky, robust black tea blend originally enjoyed by Russian travelers. Its complex flavor includes notes of dried fruit and malt.

Russian Tea - Camellia sinensis - रूसी चाय

Russian Tea is a blend of black tea with spices and citrus, offering a rich and aromatic experience reminiscent of traditional Russian tea culture.

Yunnan Tea - Camellia sinensis - युन्नान चाय

Yunnan Tea is a Chinese black tea known for its rich, malty flavor and smooth finish. It is named after the Yunnan province in China.

Oolong Tea - Camellia sinensis - ऊलौंग चाय

Oolong Tea is partially fermented, offering a flavor profile between green and black tea. It features floral and fruity notes with a smooth, mellow taste.

Pu-er Tea - Camellia sinensis - पु-एर चाय

Pu-er Tea is a fermented black tea from China, known for its earthy, mellow flavor that develops with aging. It's prized for its digestive benefits.

White Tea - Camellia sinensis - सफेद चाय

White Tea is made from young tea leaves and buds, offering a delicate, subtle flavor with light, floral notes. It's the least processed of all teas.

Yellow Tea - Camellia sinensis - येलो चाय

Yellow Tea is a rare, lightly fermented tea known for its smooth, mellow flavor and golden color. It is a delicate and sought-after variety in Chinese tea culture.

Herbal Tea - Varies by herb - हर्बल चाय

Herbal Tea is made from various herbs, flowers, fruits, and spices, offering a caffeine-free alternative with a wide range of flavors and health benefits.

Aloe Vera - Aloe barbadensis - एलोवेरा

Aloe Vera is known for its soothing and healing properties, often used in teas to support digestion and skin health.

Alfalfa - Medicago sativa - अल्फाल्फा
Alfalfa is a nutrient-rich herb used in teas for its digestive and detoxifying properties, promoting overall well-being.

Angelica - Angelica archangelica - एंजेलिका
Angelica is used in herbal teas for its digestive benefits and ability to soothe respiratory issues.

Ashwagandha - Withania somnifera - अश्वगंधा
Ashwagandha is an adaptogen known for reducing stress and enhancing overall vitality, often used in wellness teas.

Brahmi (Bacopa) - Bacopa monnieri - ब्राह्मी
Brahmi is known for its cognitive-enhancing properties, improving mental clarity and reducing stress when used in herbal teas.

Burdock - Arctium lappa - बर्डॉक
Burdock root tea is valued for its detoxifying properties and support for liver health.

Calendula - Calendula officinalis - कैलेंडुला
Calendula tea is known for its anti-inflammatory and skin-soothing properties, often used to promote overall health and wellness.

Cardamom - Elettaria cardamomum - इलायची
Cardamom tea has a warm, aromatic flavor with digestive benefits and is often used to enhance the taste of various blends.

Cinnamon - Cinnamomum verum - दारचीनी
Cinnamon tea offers a warm, sweet flavor with benefits for blood sugar regulation and digestive health.

Clove - Syzygium aromaticum - लौंग
Clove tea is known for its warming and stimulating properties, often used to support respiratory health.

Coriander - Coriandrum sativum - धनिया
Coriander tea has a mild, aromatic flavor and is used to aid digestion and relieve nausea.

Elderberry - Sambucus nigra - एल्डरबेरी
Elderberry tea is renowned for its immune-boosting properties and is often used to combat colds and flu.

Echinacea - Echinacea purpurea - एकिनेशिया
Echinacea tea is commonly used to enhance immune function and shorten the duration of colds.

Eucalyptus - Eucalyptus globulus - यूकेलिप्टस
Eucalyptus tea is used for its respiratory benefits, helping to clear congestion and soothe coughs.

Fennel - Foeniculum vulgare - सौंफ
Fennel tea has a sweet, licorice-like flavor and aids in digestion, alleviating bloating and gas.

Fenugreek - Trigonella foenum-graecum - मेथी
Fenugreek tea is used for its benefits in supporting digestion and controlling blood sugar levels.

Feverfew - Tanacetum parthenium - फीवरफ्यू
Feverfew tea is known for its anti-inflammatory properties, often used to prevent migraines and ease arthritis symptoms.

Garlic - Allium sativum - लहसुन
Garlic tea is valued for its cardiovascular benefits and immune-boosting properties.

Ginger - Zingiber officinale - अदरक
Ginger tea is a popular remedy for nausea, digestive issues, and inflammation, offering a warm, spicy flavor.

Ginkgo Biloba - Ginkgo biloba - गिन्कगो बिलोबा
Ginkgo Biloba tea is known for enhancing cognitive function and improving circulation.

Gotu Kola - Centella Asiatica - ब्राह्मी
Gotu Kola tea is used for its cognitive benefits and to promote skin health and healing.

Ginseng - Panax ginseng - जिनसेंग
Ginseng tea is an adaptogen that boosts energy, enhances mental clarity, and supports overall vitality.

Hawthorn - Crataegus monogyna - हॉथॉर्न
Hawthorn tea is used to support cardiovascular health, improving circulation and heart function.

Hyssop - Hyssopus officinalis - हयसोप
Hyssop tea has been traditionally used for its respiratory benefits and to aid digestion.

Jasmine - Jasminum spp. - चमेली
Jasmine tea blends tea leaves with jasmine flowers, offering a fragrant, floral taste and calming effects.

Lavender - Lavandula angustifolia - लैवेंडर
Lavender tea is known for its soothing and relaxing properties, often used to promote calmness and better sleep.

Lemon Balm - Melissa officinalis - नींबू बाम
Lemon Balm tea has a lemony flavor and is used to reduce anxiety and improve sleep quality.

Lemon Verbena - Aloysia citrodora - नींबू वर्बेना
Lemon Verbena tea is aromatic with a lemon-like flavor, known for its digestive and calming properties.

Lily - Lilium spp. - कुमुदनी
Lily tea is less common but is valued in some cultures for its calming effects and support of respiratory health.

Marshmallow Root - Althaea officinalis - मार्शमैलो
Marshmallow Root tea is used for its soothing effects on the digestive and respiratory systems.

Mint (Spearmint, Peppermint) - Mentha spp. - पुदीना
Mint tea, whether spearmint or peppermint, is refreshing and aids digestion, providing a cooling effect.

Mulethi (Licorice Root) - मुलैठी

Mulethi tea is used for its soothing effects on the throat and digestive system, with a sweet, licorice-like flavor.

Nettle Leaf - Urtica dioica - बिच्छू घास

Nettle Leaf tea is known for its detoxifying properties and benefits for the urinary tract and overall health.

Passion Flower - Passiflora incarnata - पैशन फ्लावर

Passion Flower tea is used to alleviate anxiety and promote restful sleep, with calming, sedative effects.

Pomegranate - Punica granatum - अनार

Pomegranate tea offers a rich, fruity flavor and is known for its antioxidant and anti-inflammatory properties.

Raspberry - Rubus idaeus - रास्पबेरी

Raspberry tea is used for its high vitamin content and potential benefits for menstrual health and digestion.

Rose - Rosa spp. - गुलाब

Rose tea is fragrant and soothing, known for its calming effects and potential benefits for skin health.

Rosehip - Rosa canina - गुलाब का फल

Rosehip tea is rich in vitamin C and antioxidants, supporting immune health and skin vitality.

Rosemary - Rosmarinus officinalis - रोजमैरी

Rosemary tea has a strong, aromatic flavor and is used for its cognitive and digestive benefits.

Sage - Salvia officinalis - सेज

Sage tea is known for its earthy flavor and is used for its anti-inflammatory and digestive properties.

Shatavari - Asparagus racemosus - शतावरी

Shatavari tea supports female reproductive health and is known for its rejuvenating and balancing properties.

Strawberry - Fragaria × ananassa - स्ट्रॉबेरी

Strawberry tea is sweet and aromatic, often enjoyed for its rich flavor and antioxidant benefits.

Tulsi - Ocimum sanctum - तुलसी

Tulsi tea, also known as Holy Basil, is revered for its adaptogenic properties, supporting stress relief and overall wellness.

Turmeric - Curcuma longa - हल्दी

Turmeric tea is known for its anti-inflammatory and antioxidant properties, supporting joint health and overall wellness.

Valerian Root - Valeriana officinalis - वैलेरियन

Valerian Root tea is used to promote relaxation and improve sleep quality, known for its calming effects.

Yarrow - Achillea millefolium - यारो

Yarrow tea is traditionally used for its anti-inflammatory and healing properties, supporting digestive and immune health

References:

Venables, M. C., Hulston, C. J., Cox, H. R., & Jeukendrup, A. E. (2008). Green tea extract ingestion, fat oxidation, and glucose tolerance in healthy humans. American Journal of Clinical Nutrition, 87(3), 778-784.

Kennedy, D. O., & Wightman, E. L. (2011). Herbal extracts and phytochemicals: Plant secondary metabolites and the enhancement of human brain function. Phytomedicine, 18(10), 857-869.

Zick, S. M., Wright, B. D., Sen, A., & Arnedt, J. T. (2011). Preliminary examination of the efficacy and safety of a standardized chamomile extract for chronic primary insomnia: A randomized placebo-controlled pilot study. BMC Complementary and Alternative Medicine, 11, 78.

Sen Sōshitsu XV. (1979). The Japanese Way of Tea: From Its Origins in China to Sen Rikyū. University of Hawaii Press.

Göbel, H., Heinze, A., Heinze-Kuhn, K., & Petersen, M. (1996). Effect of peppermint and eucalyptus oil preparations on neurophysiological and experimental algesimetric headache parameters. Journal of Pain, 67(5), 399-407.

TEA MASALA RECIPE

A Mother's Magic

My mother's tea masala is more than just a spice mix; it is a tradition, a burst of energy, and a healer of sorts. Each morning, as she prepares tea, the fragrance travels beyond the walls of our kitchen, whispering its invitation to wake up, to feel alive. Here is her cherished recipe, a secret I promised to share:

Ingredients:

100 grams of dry ginger, 100 grams of black pepper, 25 grams of cardamom, 25 grams of clove, 1 whole nutmeg

Method:

Grind the Spices: In a grinder, combine 100 grams of dry ginger, 100 grams of black pepper, 25 grams of cardamom, and 25 grams of clove. Grind them into a fine powder.

Grate the Nutmeg: Finely grate one whole nutmeg and mix it with the powdered spices.

Store the Masala: Transfer the masala into an airtight container. Store it in a cool, dry place; it will stay fresh for over six months.

This masala has been a part of my life for as long as I can remember, turning ordinary moments into extraordinary ones with just a pinch. It's more than just a recipe—it's a piece of my mother's love and care.

A gift that I now pass on to you. May it fill your home with the same warmth and joy it has always brought to mine.

"A moment to pause, like the perfect steep before the first sip."

About Author

A lifelong lover of tea, Gopal Dwivedi believes that every cup tells a story. With a deep-rooted passion for tea culture, he has explored various blends, infusions, and recipes from across the world, always looking to share his discoveries with fellow tea enthusiasts. His culinary journey began in his childhood, where tea served as a symbol of warmth, connection, and tradition in his family.

Winner of prestigious industry awards in design and innovation, Gopal approaches tea with the same creativity and detail he brings to his professional endeavors. His tea recipe book is a delightful blend of tradition, innovation, and passion. In this book, he invites readers to explore the rich and varied world of tea, from classic recipes to modern twists, all while sharing anecdotes, trivia, and personal insights.

When he's not crafting the perfect brew, Gopal enjoys diving into design curation, historical tales and experimenting with flavors that bring a sense of calm and community into everyday life. Let his recipes and stories guide you through your own tea journey, sip by sip.

Gopal Dwivedi (GD)

Author | Designer | Tea Enthusiast | Storyteller

"As this blend of recipes comes to a close, let this page steep in reflection before your next brew."

Taste Challenge
Unravel the Flavour Puzzle

Across
[3] Savory and rich, present in mushrooms and aged cheeses.
[4] Sharp and complex, found in dark chocolate and coffee.
[5] Enhances flavors, common in snacks and savory dishes.

Down
[1] Pleasing and comforting, found in fruits and desserts.
[2] Intense and spicy, from chili peppers and garlic.
[5] Tangy and refreshing, from citrus fruits and fermented foods.